Delicious Liver-Friendly Desserts: A Guide to Wholesome, Guilt-Free Sweets

Regina Bowman

Disclaimer

This book is intended to provide helpful information and recipes that support a healthy lifestyle, particularly for those interested in liver health. It is not a substitute for professional medical advice, diagnosis, or treatment. The author, Regina Bowman, is not a licensed healthcare professional, and the recipes in this book are based on personal research and general knowledge of liver-friendly ingredients and nutrition.

Before making any changes to your diet, consult with a qualified healthcare provider to determine what is appropriate for your individual health needs. If you have any known food allergies, sensitivities, or medical conditions, please carefully review the ingredients and seek personalized guidance from a healthcare professional. The author and publisher are not responsible for any adverse effects or consequences resulting from using any recipes or suggestions in this book.

TABLE OF CONTENTS

TABLE OF CONTENTS

TABLE OF CONTENTS

TABLE OF CONTENTS

Introduction

In today's dynamic environment, where lifestyle diseases like fatty liver, diabetes, and obesity are increasingly common, paying close attention to our dietary choices has never been more critical. Desserts, often viewed as indulgences or guilty pleasures, can actually be transformed into nourishing treats that support not only liver health but overall body wellness. This cookbook is designed to shift the narrative around desserts, demonstrating that it is possible to enjoy sweet dishes without compromising health or wellness goals.

THE IMPORTANCE OF HEALTHY DESSERTS FOR LIVER AND BODY WELLNESS

Your liver plays a central role in maintaining your body's overall health, acting as the body's detoxification hub, processing nutrients, and managing metabolic functions. But when burdened by poor dietary choices—particularly those high in refined sugars, unhealthy fats, and processed ingredients—it can become overwhelmed, leading to conditions like non-alcoholic fatty liver disease (NAFLD). One of the best ways to support liver function is by focusing on a clean, nutrient-dense diet, including liver-friendly desserts made from wholesome ingredients.

Healthy desserts don't have to mean deprivation. Using natural sweeteners, fiber-rich flours, and antioxidant-packed fruits, you can create delightful and satisfying treats that not only satisfy cravings but also help support your liver's detoxification processes, reduce inflammation, and promote overall metabolic health. These desserts are not just for individuals with liver concerns—they're perfect for anyone interested in maintaining a balanced, health-conscious diet.

Understanding Liver-Friendly Ingredients

Creating desserts that are not only indulgent but also beneficial for liver health involves selecting the right ingredients. By incorporating nutrient-dense, liver-supporting components, we can transform traditional sweets into functional foods that nourish the body without compromising liver function. This section delves deeper into the specific ingredients that play a pivotal role in liver-friendly desserts, focusing on their health benefits, scientific backing, and practical application in recipes.

Low-Glycemic Sweeteners

In liver-friendly desserts, managing sugar intake is critical for supporting liver health and reducing stress on the liver's detoxification processes. The goal is to use sweeteners that have a lower impact on blood glucose levels while still providing the desired sweetness. High-glycemic sweeteners and refined sugars can lead to rapid spikes in blood sugar, which in turn can increase insulin resistance and contribute to fat buildup in the liver. By incorporating low-glycemic sweeteners, we can offer a healthier alternative that provides sweetness with minimal glycemic impact.

Stevia is a plant-derived, zero-calorie sweetener that has gained popularity for its ability to provide sweetness without raising blood glucose levels. Steviol glycosides, the active compounds in stevia, are significantly sweeter than sugar. Still, they have no glycemic impact, making stevia an excellent choice for individuals managing blood sugar and liver health. Stevia can be used in many forms—powdered, liquid, or granulated—and offers the advantage of being heat-stable, so it can be used in baking or cooking without losing its sweetness.

Monk fruit sweetener is another natural, zero-calorie option that is liver-friendly due to its lack of impact on blood glucose levels. Its sweetness comes from mogrosides, compounds that are up to 250 times sweeter than sucrose. Monk fruit is free from fructose and glucose, making it particularly suitable for limiting sugar intake. Like stevia, monk fruit is available in various forms and can be used in various dessert recipes.

Erythritol, a sugar alcohol, is another low-glycemic sweetener that has little to no impact on blood glucose or insulin levels. Erythritol is unique because it is mostly absorbed by the small intestine and excreted unchanged. It bypasses metabolism in the liver and does not contribute to fat accumulation or liver stress. This makes it a highly suitable option for liver-friendly desserts. Erythritol is about 70% as sweet as sugar and can be used in baked goods or other recipes where you need a sugar substitute with minimal aftertaste.

Honey, a natural sweetener, has been praised for its health benefits, including its antioxidant, antimicrobial, and anti-inflammatory properties. However, honey has a moderate glycemic index (around 55) and consists primarily of glucose and fructose. While it contains some beneficial compounds such as flavonoids and phenolic acids, which can help reduce oxidative stress on the liver, it is still metabolized in part by the liver due to its fructose content.

The key to using honey in liver-friendly desserts is moderation. Although honey offers more nutrients than refined sugar, its glycemic impact requires careful portion control. Additionally, pairing honey with fiber-rich ingredients can help slow the absorption of sugars, reducing blood sugar spikes. For those with fatty liver or other liver concerns, small amounts of honey can be used to provide sweetness, but it's advisable to balance its use with other low-glycemic sweeteners in recipes.

Maple syrup, a natural sweetener derived from maple tree sap, contains some beneficial minerals and antioxidants, including manganese and zinc. These compounds can support overall health by providing antioxidants that help reduce oxidative stress on the liver. However, its glycemic index is moderate (around 54), meaning it can still elevate blood sugar levels, though less rapidly than refined sugars. The advantage of maple syrup in liver-friendly desserts is its richer flavor profile, allowing smaller amounts to achieve the desired sweetness. Moderation is key when using maple syrup, and pairing it with ingredients rich in fiber can help blunt its glycemic impact.

Agave syrup is known for its low glycemic index (15-30), but its high fructose content requires caution. While fructose does not cause rapid blood sugar spikes, it is metabolized almost entirely in the liver, and excessive consumption can lead to fat buildup and liver damage over time. Despite its lower glycemic index, agave syrup should be used sparingly in liver-friendly desserts. It can provide a smooth sweetness in small amounts. Still, it's important to consider alternatives like stevia or erythritol for frequent use, especially in cases where liver health is a primary concern.

Coconut sugar, with a glycemic index of 35, offers a lower-glycemic alternative to refined sugar. It contains inulin, a prebiotic fiber that helps slow the absorption of sugars and promote gut health. In addition, coconut sugar has trace minerals such as potassium and iron, adding a slight nutritional benefit. It can be a more liver-friendly option compared to refined sugars, but, like all sweeteners, it should be consumed in moderation to maintain balanced blood sugar levels and protect liver health.

Fiber-Rich Ingredients

Dietary fiber is essential for maintaining a healthy liver. It aids in digestion, supports detoxification, and helps regulate blood sugar levels. High-fiber ingredients in desserts help prevent spikes in blood glucose and support liver detox pathways by promoting the elimination of waste products and cholesterol.

Oats are rich in beta-glucan, a type of soluble fiber known for its cholesterol-lowering and anti-inflammatory properties. Soluble fiber slows the absorption of carbohydrates, preventing spikes in blood sugar, which is critical for liver health. Additionally, oats help reduce the amount of cholesterol and fat circulating in the bloodstream, which can lower the risk of fat buildup in the liver.

Chia seeds are a nutrient powerhouse, packed with fiber, omega-3 fatty acids, and antioxidants. Their high fiber content supports digestion and prevents constipation, which helps the liver efficiently eliminate toxins from the body. Chia seeds also help stabilize blood sugar levels, further supporting liver function by reducing insulin resistance.

Like chia seeds, **flaxseeds** are an excellent source of fiber and omega-3s. They also contain lignans, phytonutrients that have been shown to support liver health by reducing inflammation and improving liver function in cases of fatty liver disease. Ground flaxseeds can be added to baked goods or used as an egg substitute to boost fiber and omega-3 content.

Almond flour is a low-carbohydrate, high-fiber alternative to wheat flour. Rich in healthy fats, fiber, and protein, it provides a slow release of energy, making it ideal for managing blood sugar levels and reducing the liver's metabolic burden. Almond flour also offers vitamin E, an antioxidant that helps protect liver cells from oxidative stress.

Antioxidant-Packed Fruits and Nuts

Antioxidants protect liver cells from oxidative stress, significantly contributing to liver damage and inflammation. Incorporating antioxidant-rich fruits and nuts into desserts can enhance the nutritional profile and actively support liver function.

Berries are some of the most antioxidant-dense fruits, particularly rich in anthocyanins, which have been shown to reduce oxidative stress and inflammation in the liver. Studies suggest that regular consumption of berries can reduce fat accumulation and improve liver function markers in individuals with fatty liver disease.

Cacao is one of the richest sources of flavonoids, potent antioxidants that protect against liver cell damage and reduce inflammation. Dark chocolate with high cacao content (70% or higher) is not only indulgent but also beneficial for liver health. Including cacao in desserts like mousse, energy balls, or pudding can provide a rich source of antioxidants.

Citrus Fruits (Oranges, Lemons, Grapefruit) contain vitamin C and flavonoids that support detoxification. These fruits can add zest and flavor to cakes, muffins, and parfaits while promoting liver enzyme production.

Walnuts are particularly beneficial for liver health due to their high omega-3 fatty acid content and antioxidants like polyphenols. Research has shown that walnuts help reduce fat accumulation in the liver and improve liver function in individuals with NAFLD. Adding walnuts to baked goods or energy bites boosts both flavor and nutrition.

Pistachios are rich in antioxidants, particularly gamma-tocopherol, a form of vitamin E that has been shown to reduce oxidative stress and inflammation in the liver. Their high fiber content and healthy fats also support metabolic health, making them an ideal ingredient in liver-friendly desserts like nut-based crusts, energy balls, or toppings for chia puddings and parfaits.

Almonds provide vitamin E, a potent antioxidant that helps protect liver cells from damage. Ground into flour, they can be used in cakes and cookies, or added as a topping for a boost of healthy fats and protein.

By prioritizing these liver-supportive ingredients, you can create desserts that not only satisfy cravings but also contribute to liver health and overall well-being. These ingredients offer a combination of flavor, nutrition, and therapeutic benefits, allowing you to enjoy desserts without compromising liver function.

How to Enjoy Desserts Without Guilt

Desserts often come with feelings of guilt, especially for those trying to follow a liver-friendly or health-conscious diet. However, this guilt is unnecessary when you choose the right ingredients and understand their impact on the body. By avoiding refined sugars, opting for natural, low-glycemic sweeteners, and emphasizing fiber and antioxidants, you can enjoy desserts in a way that nourishes rather than depletes your body.

This book is not about restriction but balance and making wise choices. Whether managing liver health, reducing sugar intake, or simply seeking wholesome alternatives, these desserts allow you to indulge mindfully. You can have your sweet moments while supporting both your liver and your overall well-being.

Dessert Recipes

Coconut Milk Panna Cotta with Raspberry Sauce

PREP TIME
15 MIN

CHILL TIME
4 HOURS

YIELD
4 SERVINGS

Instructions:

1. In a saucepan, warm the coconut milk over medium heat.
2. Sprinkle the gelatin over 2 tablespoons of water in a small bowl and let sit for 5 minutes to bloom.
3. Once the coconut milk is warm, whisk in the gelatin until fully dissolved.
4. Add the stevia and vanilla extract, and whisk until smooth.
5. Pour the mixture into individual ramekins and refrigerate for at least 4 hours until set.
6. For the raspberry sauce, blend the fresh raspberries and strain to remove seeds. Add a few drops of stevia if desired.
7. Serve the panna cotta with raspberry sauce drizzled on top.

Ingredients:

- 2 cups full-fat coconut milk
- 1 1/2 teaspoons gelatin
- 1/8 teaspoon stevia (or monk fruit sweetener, to taste)
- 1 teaspoon vanilla extract
- 1 cup fresh raspberries

Tips:
- If you prefer agar-agar, you can substitute it for gelatin to make this dish vegan.
- You can also use blueberries or strawberries for the sauce instead of raspberries.
- Adjust the sweetness level based on personal preference.

Nutrition per Serving:

- Calories: 200
- Protein: 3g
- Carbohydrates: 10g
- Fat: 18g
- Fiber: 2g
- Sodium: 10mg
- Potassium: 250mg

Almond Flour Brownies

 PREP TIME
10 MIN

 **COOK TIME**
20-25 MIN

 **YIELD**
12 BROWNIES

Instructions:

1. Preheat the oven to 350°F (175°C) and grease an 8x8-inch baking pan.
2. Mix the almond flour, cocoa powder, erythritol, and baking soda in a bowl.
3. Whisk together the eggs, melted coconut oil, and vanilla extract in another bowl.
4. Combine the wet and dry ingredients, stirring until smooth.
5. Pour the batter into the prepared baking pan and smooth the top.
6. Bake for 20-25 minutes until a toothpick inserted into the center comes out clean.
7. Let cool before slicing into squares.

Tips:
- You can replace erythritol with 1/8 teaspoon stevia for a more concentrated sweetener option.
- If you prefer a fudgier texture, reduce the baking time slightly.
- Add a handful of chopped nuts or dark chocolate chips for extra flavor.

Ingredients:

- 1 1/2 cups almond flour
- 1/4 cup unsweetened cocoa powder
- 1/4 cup erythritol (or monk fruit sweetener, 1:1 ratio)
- 1/2 teaspoon baking soda
- 2 large eggs
- 1/4 cup coconut oil, melted
- 1 teaspoon vanilla extract

Nutrition per brownie:

- Calories: 140
- Protein: 4g
- Carbohydrates: 6g
- Fat: 12g
- Fiber: 2g
- Sodium: 60mg
- Potassium: 120mg

Grilled Peaches with Coconut Cream

 PREP TIME
5 MIN

 COOK TIME
3-4 MIN

 YIELD
4 SERVINGS

Ingredients:

- 4 ripe peaches, halved and pitted
- 1/4 cup coconut cream
- 1/8 teaspoon stevia (optional, depending on sweetness of peaches)
- 1/2 teaspoon vanilla extract
- Fresh mint leaves for garnish (optional)

Nutrition per Serving:

Calories: 120| Protein: 1g |
Carbohydrates:15g | Fat: 7g | Fiber:3g |
Sodium: 5mg | Potassium: 300mg

Instructions:

1. Preheat a grill to medium heat.
2. Grill the peach halves, cut side down, for 3-4 minutes until caramelized and tender.
3. While grilling, whisk the coconut cream with stevia and vanilla extract until smooth.
4. Serve the grilled peaches with a dollop of coconut cream and garnish with fresh mint leaves.

Tips:

- You can omit the stevia entirely if your peaches are very ripe and sweet.
- For an added crunch, sprinkle chopped nuts like almonds or pecans on top.
- This dessert also works well with grilled nectarines or plums.

Avocado Chocolate Mousse

 PREP TIME
10 MIN

 CHILL TIME
30 MIN

 YIELD
2 SERVINGS

Ingredients:

- 2 ripe avocados
- 1/4 cup unsweetened cocoa powder
- 1/4 cup almond milk (or any plant-based milk)
- 1/8 teaspoon liquid stevia (or monk fruit sweetener, to taste)
- 1 teaspoon vanilla extract
- Pinch of salt

Nutrition per Serving:

Calories: 180 | Protein: 3g |
Carbohydrates: 12g | Fat: 15g | Fiber: 7g |
Sodium: 50mg | Potassium: 600mg

Instructions:

1. Scoop out the flesh from the avocados and place in a blender or food processor.
2. Add the cocoa powder, almond milk, vanilla extract, stevia, and a pinch of salt.
3. Blend until smooth and creamy.
4. Taste and adjust sweetness by adding more stevia, if needed.
5. Chill in the fridge for at least 30 minutes before serving.

Tips:

- For extra richness, you can add 1 tablespoon of coconut cream to the mousse.
- Substitute almond milk with coconut milk for a creamier texture.
- Garnish with fresh berries or a sprinkle of cacao nibs for added texture.

Banana Oat Cookies

 PREP TIME 10 MIN

 **COOK TIME** 10-12 MIN

 **YIELD** 12 COOKIES

Instructions:

1. Preheat the oven to 350°F (175°C) and line a baking sheet with parchment paper.
2. In a bowl, mash the bananas until smooth.
3. Add the oats, cinnamon, and stevia (if using) and mix well. Stir in raisins if desired.
4. Scoop small mounds of the batter onto the prepared baking sheet.
5. Flatten slightly and bake for 10-12 minutes until golden and set.
6. Let cool on a wire rack before serving.

Ingredients:

- 2 ripe bananas, mashed
- 1 1/2 cups rolled oats
- 1/2 teaspoon cinnamon
- 1/8 teaspoon liquid stevia (optional, for added sweetness)
- 1/4 cup raisins (optional)

Nutrition per cookie:

- Calories: 85
- Protein: 2g
- Carbohydrates: 17g
- Fat: 1g
- Fiber: 2g
- Sodium: 1mg
- Potassium: 120mg

Tips:
- Omit stevia if the bananas are very ripe, as they'll provide enough sweetness.
- Add chopped walnuts or dark chocolate chips for variation.
- Store leftovers in an airtight container for up to 3 days.

Frozen Yogurt Bark with Berries

 PREP TIME
10 MIN

 FREEZING TIME:
2 HOURS

YIELD
4 SERVINGS

Ingredients:

- 2 cups plain Greek yogurt
- 1 tablespoon honey or maple syrup
- 1 cup mixed berries (blueberries, raspberries, strawberries)
- 2 tablespoons chia seeds or flaxseeds
- ¼ cup granola (optional)

Nutrition per Serving:

- Calories: 90
- Protein: 8g
- Carbohydrates: 11g
- Fats: 2g
- Fiber: 2g
- Cholesterol: 5mg
- Sodium: 30mg
- Potassium: 180mg

Instructions:

1. Mix the Greek yogurt and honey or maple syrup in a bowl until well combined.
2. Line a baking sheet with parchment paper and spread the yogurt mixture evenly to about ½-inch thickness.
3. Sprinkle the berries, chia seeds, and granola (if using) over the yogurt.
4. Place the baking sheet in the freezer for at least 2 hours or until completely frozen.
5. Break into pieces and serve.

Tips:
- Use coconut yogurt for a dairy-free version.
- Swap berries with sliced mango, kiwi, or pomegranate seeds for variety.
- Add shredded coconut or dark chocolate chips for extra flavor.

Orange and Almond Cake

 PREP TIME 15 MIN  **COOK TIME** 45 MIN  **YIELD** 8 SERVINGS

Instructions:

1. Preheat the oven to 350°F (175°C). Grease and line an 8-inch round cake pan.
2. Boil the oranges (whole, skin on) in water for 30 minutes. Drain and let them cool.
3. Blend the oranges (with peel) in a blender until smooth.
4. Mix almond flour, coconut sugar, baking powder, and vanilla extract in a bowl. Add the blended oranges and eggs, and stir to combine.
5. Pour the batter into the prepared pan and top with slivered almonds.
6. Bake for 45 minutes or until a toothpick inserted into the center comes out clean.
7. Cool before serving.

Tips:
- Replace almond flour with coconut flour for a lower-carb version (adjust the amount as needed).
- Use lemon zest instead of oranges for a different citrus flavor.
- Add a teaspoon of cinnamon for a warm, spicy kick.

Ingredients:

- 2 large oranges
- 1½ cups almond flour
- ½ cup coconut sugar
- 3 eggs
- 1 teaspoon baking powder
- 1 teaspoon vanilla extract
- ¼ cup slivered almonds for topping

Nutrition per Serving:

- Calories: 220
- Protein: 6g
- Carbohydrates: 21g
- Fats: 12g
- Fiber: 4g
- Cholesterol: 55mg
- Sodium: 40mg
- Potassium: 230mg

Coconut Yogurt Parfait

 PREP TIME
5 MIN

 YIELD
4 SERVINGS

Instructions:

1. Layer coconut yogurt, granola, and berries in serving cups or glasses.
2. Sprinkle chia seeds on top and drizzle with honey, if desired.
3. Serve immediately or refrigerate for later.

Tips:
- Replace coconut yogurt with Greek yogurt for a higher protein option.
- Use sliced bananas, peaches, or pineapple in place of berries.
- Swap granola for chopped nuts or seeds for a grain-free version.

Ingredients:
- 2 cups coconut yogurt
- 1 cup granola
- 1 cup mixed berries (strawberries, blueberries, raspberries)
- 2 tablespoons chia seeds
- 1 tablespoon honey or maple syrup (optional)

Nutrition per Serving:
Calories: 190 | Protein: 3g | Carbohydrates: 28g | Fats: 8g | Fiber: 5g | Cholesterol: 0mg | Sodium: 20mg | Potassium: 150mg

Papaya and Lime Sorbet

 PREP TIME
10 MINUTES

 FREEZING TIME:
4 HOURS

 YIELD
4 SERVINGS

Instructions:

1. Blend papaya, lime juice, honey, and coconut water in a blender until smooth.
2. Pour the mixture into a shallow container and freeze for 4 hours, stirring occasionally.
3. Serve in bowls or scooped into small glasses.

Tips:
- Replace papaya with mango or cantaloupe for a different flavor.
- If you prefer a sweeter sorbet, add banana or extra honey.
- Use lemon juice instead of lime for a tangy twist.

Ingredients:
- 2 cups fresh papaya, peeled, seeded, and cubed
- ¼ cup fresh lime juice
- 2 tablespoons honey or maple syrup (optional)
- 1 tablespoon coconut water

Nutrition per Serving:
Calories: 60 | Protein: 1g | Carbohydrates:15g | Fats: 0g | Fiber: 2g | Cholesterol: 0mg | Sodium: 3mg | Potassium: 230mg

Date and Walnut Bites

 PREP TIME
10 MIN

 CHILL TIME
20 MIN

 YIELD
12 BITES

Instructions:

1. Blend dates, walnuts, cocoa powder, coconut oil, vanilla extract, and salt in a food processor until the mixture forms a sticky dough.
2. Roll the dough into small bite-sized balls.
3. Place the bites on a parchment-lined tray and freeze for 20 minutes to firm up.
4. Serve chilled or at room temperature.

Ingredients:

- 1 cup Medjool dates, pitted
- ½ cup walnuts
- 2 tablespoons unsweetened cocoa powder
- 1 tablespoon coconut oil
- 1 teaspoon vanilla extract
- Pinch of sea salt

Nutrition per bite:

- Calories: 80
- Protein: 1g
- Carbohydrates: 11g
- Fats: 4g
- Fiber: 2g
- Cholesterol: 0mg
- Sodium: 12mg
- Potassium: 160mg

Tips:
- Replace walnuts with almonds or pecans for a different flavor.
- Swap cocoa powder for carob powder for a caffeine-free version.
- Add a handful of shredded coconut for extra texture and flavor.

Stewed Cinnamon Apples

 **PREP TIME** 5 MIN  **COOK TIME** 10 MIN  **YIELD** 4 SERVINGS

Instructions:

1. Heat coconut oil in a medium saucepan over medium heat.
2. Add sliced apples, maple syrup, cinnamon, nutmeg, and water.
3. Cook for 8-10 minutes, stirring occasionally, until apples are tender and fragrant.
4. Serve warm on its own or with a dollop of coconut yogurt.

Tips:
- Replace apples with pears or peaches for variety.
- Use honey instead of maple syrup for a different sweetener.
- Add raisins or dried cranberries for extra texture.

Ingredients:
- 4 medium apples, peeled, cored, and sliced
- 1 tablespoon coconut oil
- 1 tablespoon maple syrup
- 1 teaspoon ground cinnamon
- ½ teaspoon ground nutmeg (optional)
- ½ cup water

Nutrition per Serving:
Calories: 120 | Protein: 0g | Carbohydrates:28g | Fats: 2g | Fiber: 4g | Cholesterol: 0mg | Sodium: 0mg | Potassium: 220mg

---

Mango Chia Pudding

 PREP TIME 10 MINUTES   **CHILL TIME:** 4 HOURS   **YIELD** 4 SERVINGS

Instructions:

1. Whisk together mango puree, almond milk, maple syrup (if using), and vanilla extract in a bowl.
2. Stir in chia seeds and mix well.
3. Cover and refrigerate for 4 hours or overnight, stirring occasionally to prevent clumping.
4. Serve chilled, topped with fresh mango chunks or shredded coconut.

Tips:
- Replace mango with pineapple or peach puree for different flavors.
- Use coconut milk instead of almond milk for a richer texture.
- Add a pinch of turmeric for an extra health boost.

Ingredients:
- 1 cup mango puree (from fresh or frozen mango)
- 1 cup almond milk (or any plant-based milk)
- ¼ cup chia seeds
- 1 tablespoon maple syrup (optional)
- 1 teaspoon vanilla extract

Nutrition per Serving:
Calories: 160 | Protein: 3g | Carbohydrates: 25g | Fats: 6g | Fiber: 6g | Cholesterol: 0mg | Sodium: 25mg | Potassium: 190mg

Oat and Apple Crisp

 PREP TIME
15 MIN

 COOK TIME
30 MIN

 YIELD
4 SERVINGS

Instructions:

1. Preheat oven to 350°F (175°C).
2. Toss sliced apples with lemon juice, 1 tablespoon of maple syrup, and cinnamon. Spread evenly in a baking dish.
3. Mix oats, almond flour, melted coconut oil, and honey or maple syrup in a bowl. Add nutmeg if using.
4. Sprinkle the oat mixture evenly over the apples.
5. Bake for 25-30 minutes or until the topping is golden brown and the apples are tender.
6. Serve warm, optionally with a scoop of coconut yogurt or a drizzle of almond butter.

Tips:
- Replace apples with pears or peaches for a different flavor.
- Use coconut sugar instead of maple syrup for a lower glycemic option.
- Substitute almond flour with oat flour or another gluten-free flour.

Ingredients:
- 4 medium apples, peeled, cored, and sliced
- 1 tablespoon lemon juice
- 1 tablespoon maple syrup
- 1 teaspoon cinnamon
- 1 cup rolled oats
- ¼ cup almond flour
- 2 tablespoons coconut oil, melted
- 1 tablespoon honey or maple syrup
- ¼ teaspoon nutmeg (optional)

Nutrition per Serving:

- Calories: 190
- Protein: 2g
- Carbohydrates: 33g
- Fats: 6g
- Fiber: 5g
- Cholesterol: 0mg
- Sodium: 3mg
- Potassium: 250mg

Chocolate-Dipped Bananas

 PREP TIME **5 MIN**   CHILL TIME: **1 HOUR**   YIELD **4 SERVINGS**

Instructions:

1. Melt the dark chocolate chips and coconut oil in a microwave-safe bowl, stirring until smooth.
2. Dip each banana half into the melted chocolate, then place on a parchment-lined baking sheet.
3. Sprinkle with chopped nuts and shredded coconut if desired.
4. Freeze for 1 hour or until fully hardened. Serve cold.

Ingredients:

- 2 bananas, cut into halves
- ½ cup dark chocolate chips (70% cocoa or higher)
- 1 tablespoon coconut oil
- 2 tablespoons chopped nuts (almonds, walnuts, or pistachios)
- 1 tablespoon shredded coconut (optional)

Nutrition per Serving:

Calories: 160 | Protein: 2g | Carbohydrates: 24g | Fats: 8g | Fiber: 4g | Cholesterol: 0mg | Sodium: 2mg | Potassium: 300mg

Tips:
- Use milk chocolate or white chocolate if you prefer a sweeter taste.
- Swap bananas with strawberries or kiwi slices.
- For a nut-free version, use chia seeds or sunflower seeds as toppings.

Frozen Kiwi Pops

 PREP TIME **10 MINUTES**    FREEZING TIME: **4 HOURS**   YIELD **8 POPS**

Instructions:

1. Blend half the kiwis with coconut water, honey, and lime juice until smooth.
2. Pour the mixture into popsicle molds and place kiwi slices into each mold.
3. Freeze for at least 4 hours until firm.
4. Serve straight from the freezer for a refreshing treat.

Ingredients:

- 4 kiwis, peeled and sliced
- 1 cup coconut water
- 1 tablespoon honey or maple syrup (optional)
- 1 tablespoon lime juice

Nutrition per pop:

Calories: 30 | Protein: 0g | Carbohydrates: 8g | Fats: 0g | Fiber: 2g | Cholesterol:0mg | Sodium: 5mg | Potassium: 110mg

Tips:
- Replace kiwis with watermelon or pineapple for a different fruit pop.
- Add a bit of mint or basil to the blender for a refreshing twist.
- Swap coconut water with orange juice for a more citrusy flavor.

Matcha Green Tea Energy Balls

 PREP TIME
10 MIN

 COOK TIME
NONE

 YIELD
12 BALLS

Instructions:

1. In a food processor, pulse the almonds until coarsely chopped.
2. Add the dates, shredded coconut, matcha powder, chia seeds, almond butter, vanilla extract, and a pinch of salt.
3. Process until the mixture sticks together and forms a dough-like consistency.
4. Roll the mixture into 1-inch balls. You can dust them with extra matcha powder or coconut if desired.
5. Store the energy balls in an airtight container in the fridge for up to a week.

Tips:
- If the mixture is too dry, add a teaspoon of water or extra nut butter.
- For extra sweetness, add a small amount of maple syrup or honey.
- You can swap almonds for cashews, walnuts, or other nuts, and add a handful of chocolate chips or goji berries for variety.
- Add protein powder for an extra protein boost.

Ingredients:

- 1 cup pitted Medjool dates
- 1/2 cup almonds (or any nut of choice)
- 1/2 cup shredded coconut (unsweetened)
- 1 tablespoon matcha powder
- 1 tablespoon chia seeds (optional for added fiber)
- 1 tablespoon almond butter (or any nut butter)
- 1 teaspoon vanilla extract
- Pinch of salt

Nutrition per ball:
- Calories: 95
- Protein: 2g
- Carbohydrates: 11g
- Fat: 5g
- Fiber: 2g
- Sugars: 8g
- Sodium: 20mg
- Potassium: 130mg

Beet and Chocolate Cake (Gluten-Free)

 PREP TIME 15 MIN  **COOK TIME** 40 MIN  **YIELD** 8 SERVINGS

Instructions:

1. Preheat the oven to 350°F (175°C) and grease a round cake pan.
2. Whisk together the beet purée, eggs, coconut sugar, and vanilla extract in a large bowl.
3. Mix the almond flour, cocoa powder, baking powder, and sea salt in a separate bowl.
4. Combine the wet and dry ingredients, stirring until smooth. Fold in the dark chocolate chips, if using.
5. Pour the batter into the prepared cake pan and bake for 35-40 minutes, or until a toothpick inserted into the center comes out clean.
6. Let cool before slicing and serving.

Ingredients:

- 1 cup cooked beets, puréed
- 1 cup almond flour
- ½ cup cocoa powder
- ½ cup coconut sugar or maple syrup
- 3 eggs
- 1 teaspoon vanilla extract
- 1 teaspoon baking powder
- ½ teaspoon sea salt
- ¼ cup dark chocolate chips (optional)

Nutrition per Serving:

- Calories: 190
- Protein: 6g
- Carbohydrates: 22g
- Fats: 9g
- Fiber: 5g
- Cholesterol: 55mg
- Sodium: 125mg
- Potassium: 250mg

Tips:

- Swap beet purée with pumpkin purée or mashed sweet potato for a slightly different flavor.
- Use agave syrup or date syrup instead of coconut sugar.
- Replace almond flour with hazelnut flour for a nutty twist.

Sweet Potato and Ginger Cheesecake (Vegan)

 PREP TIME **20 MIN**

 COOK TIME **20 MIN**

CHILL TIME **2 HOURS**

YIELD **8 SERVINGS**

Instructions:

1. Preheat the oven to 350°F (175°C). Grease a springform pan.
2. Prepare the crust by blending the oats, almonds, coconut oil, and maple syrup in a food processor until crumbly. Press into the bottom of the springform pan.
3. Bake the crust for 10 minutes, then set aside to cool.
4. Combine the sweet potato, coconut cream, maple syrup, ginger, vanilla extract, and cinnamon in a blender until smooth.
5. Pour the filling over the cooled crust and smooth out the top.
6. Bake for 30-35 minutes, until set. Cool completely, then refrigerate for at least 2 hours before serving.

Tips:
- Use canned pumpkin instead of sweet potato for a smoother texture.
- Replace ginger with nutmeg or cardamom for a different spice profile.
- Add a date syrup drizzle on top for extra sweetness.

Ingredients:

Crust:
- 1 cup oats
- ½ cup almonds or walnuts
- 2 tablespoons coconut oil, melted
- 2 tablespoons maple syrup

Filling:
- 1 cup mashed sweet potato (cooked and cooled)
- ½ cup coconut cream
- ¼ cup maple syrup
- 1 tablespoon grated fresh ginger
- 1 teaspoon vanilla extract
- 1 teaspoon cinnamon

Nutrition per Serving:

- Calories: 260
- Protein: 4g
- Carbohydrates: 38g
- Fats: 10g
- Fiber: 5g
- Cholesterol: 0mg
- Sodium: 25mg
- Potassium: 300mg

Quinoa and Apple Cinnamon Bake

 PREP TIME
15 MIN

 COOK TIME
35 MIN

 YIELD
6 SERVINGS

Ingredients:

- 1 cup quinoa, rinsed
- 1 ½ cups unsweetened almond milk
- 2 apples, peeled, cored, and chopped
- 2 tablespoons maple syrup
- 1 teaspoon cinnamon
- 1 teaspoon vanilla extract
- ¼ cup chopped walnuts (optional)

Nutrition per Serving:

- Calories: 200
- Protein: 5g
- Carbohydrates: 34g
- Fats: 6g
- Fiber: 4g
- Cholesterol: 0mg
- Sodium: 30mg
- Potassium: 320mg

Instructions:

1. Preheat the oven to 350°F (175°C) and grease a baking dish.
2. Combine the quinoa, almond milk, chopped apples, maple syrup, cinnamon, and vanilla extract in a large bowl. Stir to mix well.
3. Pour the mixture into the prepared baking dish and spread evenly. Top with chopped walnuts, if using.
4. Bake for 30-35 minutes, or until the quinoa is tender and the top is golden.
5. Let cool slightly before serving.

Tips:
- Use pears instead of apples for a different fruit profile.
- Swap maple syrup with honey for a different sweetener.
- Replace walnuts with pecans or omit them for a nut-free version.

Sweet Corn and Coconut Pudding

⏱ PREP TIME
10 MIN

🔲 COOK TIME
20 MIN

🍽 YIELD
4 SERVINGS

Instructions:

1. In a blender, blend the corn kernels and coconut milk until smooth.
2. Combine the blended corn mixture, honey, vanilla, and cinnamon in a saucepan. Cook over medium heat, stirring occasionally, for 10-15 minutes until slightly thickened.
3. If using cornstarch, mix it with 2 tablespoons of water to form a slurry. Add to the saucepan and cook for another 5 minutes, stirring constantly until thickened.
4. Serve warm or chilled, topped with a sprinkle of cinnamon or shredded coconut.

Ingredients:

- 1 ½ cups fresh or frozen corn kernels
- 1 can full-fat coconut milk (13.5 oz)
- 2 tablespoons honey or maple syrup
- 1 teaspoon vanilla extract
- ¼ teaspoon cinnamon
- 1 tablespoon cornstarch (optional, for thickening)

Nutrition per Serving:

- Calories: 220
- Protein: 3g
- Carbohydrates: 26g
- Fats: 14g
- Fiber: 2g
- Cholesterol: 0mg
- Sodium: 20mg
- Potassium: 180mg

Tips:
- Replace honey with agave syrup or coconut sugar for different sweeteners.
- Add a pinch of nutmeg for extra warmth in the flavor.
- Use almond milk instead of coconut milk for a lighter texture (though it may be less rich).

Lemon Blueberry Parfait

 PREP TIME
10 MIN

 YIELD
2 SERVINGS

Instructions:

1. Mix the yogurt, honey, and lemon zest in a small bowl until well combined.
2. Layer the yogurt mixture and blueberries in serving glasses or bowls, alternating between the two.
3. Top with granola for added crunch, if desired, and serve immediately.

Tips:
- Replace blueberries with raspberries or strawberries for a different berry flavor.
- Use chia seeds instead of granola for added fiber.
- Swap Greek yogurt with coconut yogurt for a dairy-free option.

Ingredients:

- 1 cup Greek yogurt (or coconut yogurt)
- 1 tablespoon honey or maple syrup
- ½ teaspoon lemon zest
- ½ cup fresh blueberries
- 2 tablespoons granola (optional)

Nutrition per Serving:

Calories: 150 | Protein: 8g | Carbohydrates: 25g | Fats: 4g | Fiber: 3g | Cholesterol: 5mg | Sodium: 40mg | Potassium: 250mg

Coconut Matcha Ice Cream

 PREP TIME
10 MINUTES

 FREEZING TIME
4 HOURS

 YIELD
4 SERVINGS

Instructions:

1. Combine coconut milk, honey (or maple syrup), matcha powder, vanilla extract, and sea salt in a blender. Blend until smooth.
2. Pour the mixture into an ice cream maker and churn according to the manufacturer's instructions. If you don't have an ice cream maker, pour the mixture into a shallow dish and freeze, stirring every 30 minutes for 2-3 hours until creamy.
3. Once frozen, serve the ice cream in bowls or cones, and enjoy!

Tips:
- Replace honey with agave syrup or coconut sugar for different sweetness levels.
- Add coconut flakes or dark chocolate shavings for extra texture.
- Use almond milk instead of coconut milk for a lighter version (though it will be less creamy).

Ingredients:

- 1 can full-fat coconut milk (13.5 oz)
- 2 tablespoons honey or maple syrup
- 1 tablespoon matcha green tea powder
- 1 teaspoon vanilla extract
- 1 pinch of sea salt

Nutrition per Serving:

Calories: 180 | Protein: 1g | Carbohydrates: 14g | Fats: 14g | Fiber: 1g | Cholesterol: 0mg | Sodium: 35mg | Potassium: 220mg

Lavender Honey Almond Cake

 PREP TIME 15 MIN    **COOK TIME** 25 MIN    **YIELD** 8 SERVINGS

Instructions:

1. Preheat the oven to 350°F (175°C) and grease a round cake pan.
2. Whisk together the eggs, honey, vanilla extract, and melted coconut oil in a large bowl.
3. Combine the almond flour, coconut flour, baking powder, sea salt, and dried lavender in a separate bowl.
4. Gradually add the dry ingredients to the wet ingredients, stirring until well combined.
5. Pour the batter into the prepared cake pan and bake for 20-25 minutes, or until a toothpick comes out clean.
6. Let cool before serving.

Ingredients:

- 1 cup almond flour
- ¼ cup coconut flour
- 3 eggs
- ¼ cup honey
- 1 teaspoon dried lavender
- 1 teaspoon vanilla extract
- 1 teaspoon baking powder
- ¼ cup coconut oil, melted
- ¼ teaspoon sea salt

Tips:
- Replace lavender with lemon zest for a citrusy flavor.
- Swap honey with maple syrup for a different sweetness profile.
- Use olive oil instead of coconut oil for a more savory note.

Nutrition per Serving:

- Calories: 210
- Protein: 5g
- Carbohydrates: 17g
- Fats: 15g
- Fiber: 4g
- Cholesterol: 55mg
- Sodium: 150mg
- Potassium: 90mg

Peanut Butter and Oat Energy Bars

 PREP TIME
10 MIN

 CHILL TIME
1 HOUR

YIELD
8 SERVINGS

Instructions:

1. In a medium mixing bowl, combine the oats, ground flaxseeds, chia seeds, and shredded coconut (if using).
2. In a small saucepan, warm peanut butter, honey or maple syrup, and vanilla extract over low heat until well combined and smooth.
3. Pour the peanut butter mixture over the dry ingredients and mix thoroughly.
4. Press the mixture into a parchment-lined 8x8-inch pan and refrigerate for 1 hour until set.
5. Once firm, cut into 8 bars and enjoy.

Ingredients:

- 1 cup rolled oats
- ½ cup natural peanut butter (no added sugar)
- ¼ cup honey or maple syrup
- ¼ cup ground flaxseeds
- 1 teaspoon vanilla extract
- 2 tablespoons chia seeds
- ¼ cup unsweetened shredded coconut (optional)
- 2 tablespoons dark chocolate chips (optional)

Nutrition per Serving:

- Calories: 210
- Protein: 6g
- Carbohydrates: 24g
- Fats: 12g
- Fiber: 5g
- Cholesterol: 0mg
- Sodium: 30mg
- Potassium: 140mg

Tips:

- Swap peanut butter for almond butter or cashew butter for a different flavor.
- Use agave syrup instead of honey for a vegan version.
- Add dried fruit like cranberries or raisins for extra sweetness.

Coconut Macaroons

 PREP TIME **10 MIN** COOK TIME **20 MIN** YIELD **10 MACAROONS**

Instructions:

1. Preheat the oven to 350°F (175°C). Line a baking sheet with parchment paper.
2. Mix shredded coconut, coconut flour, coconut oil, maple syrup, vanilla extract, and sea salt in a bowl until well combined.
3. Scoop small portions of the mixture and form into balls. Place on the baking sheet.
4. Bake for 15-20 minutes until golden brown on top.
5. Cool completely before serving.

Tips:
- Replace coconut oil with almond butter for a richer taste.
- Swap maple syrup for honey or agave nectar for a different sweetener.
- Add cocoa powder for a chocolatey twist.

Ingredients:

- 1½ cups shredded unsweetened coconut
- ¼ cup coconut flour
- 2 tablespoons coconut oil, melted
- ¼ cup maple syrup
- 1 teaspoon vanilla extract
- Pinch of sea salt

Nutrition per macaroon:

- Calories: 110
- Protein: 1g
- Carbohydrates: 7g
- Fats: 9g
- Fiber: 3g
- Cholesterol: 0mg
- Sodium: 10mg
- Potassium: 60mg

Peach and Almond Crumble

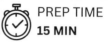 PREP TIME
15 MIN

 COOK TIME
30 MIN

 YIELD
6 SERVINGS

Instructions:

1. Preheat the oven to 350°F (175°C).
2. Toss peaches with maple syrup and cinnamon in a baking dish.
3. Mix almond flour, sliced almonds, coconut oil, and sea salt in a bowl. Sprinkle over the peaches.
4. Bake for 25-30 minutes, until the topping is golden and the peaches are bubbly.
5. Serve warm with a scoop of coconut yogurt.

Tips:
- Replace peaches with plums or pears.
- Use oats instead of almond flour for a more traditional crumble texture.
- Add a dash of nutmeg for extra warmth.

Ingredients:

- 4 ripe peaches, sliced
- 2 tablespoons maple syrup
- 1 teaspoon cinnamon
- 1 cup almond flour
- ¼ cup sliced almonds
- 2 tablespoons coconut oil, melted
- Pinch of sea salt

Nutrition per Serving:

Calories: 180 | Protein: 3g | Carbohydrates: 20g | Fats: 11g | Fiber: 3g | Cholesterol: 0mg | Sodium: 25mg | Potassium: 240mg

---

Berry Sorbet

 PREP TIME
5 MIN

 FREEZING TIME
2 HOURS

 YIELD
4 SERVINGS

Instructions:

1. Blend berries, honey, lemon juice, and water in a blender or food processor until smooth.
2. Pour the mixture into a shallow dish and freeze for 1-2 hours, stirring occasionally to prevent ice crystals from forming.
3. Scoop into bowls and serve chilled.

Tips:
- Swap berries with mango, pineapple, or peaches for a tropical sorbet.
- Add a handful of fresh mint leaves for an extra refreshing flavor.
- Use coconut water instead of water for added electrolytes.

Ingredients:

- 2 cups mixed berries (blueberries, raspberries, strawberries)
- 2 tablespoons honey or maple syrup (optional)
- 1 tablespoon lemon juice
- ½ cup water

Nutrition per Serving:

Calories: 60 | Protein: 1g | Carbohydrates:15g | Fats: 0g | Fiber: 4g | Cholesterol: 0mg | Sodium: 0mg | Potassium: 150mg

Orange and Olive Oil Cake

 **PREP TIME** 15 MIN  **COOK TIME** 40 MIN  **YIELD** 8 SERVINGS

Instructions:

1. Preheat the oven to 350°F (175°C). Grease and line a round cake pan.
2. In a large bowl, whisk together the olive oil, date syrup, eggs, orange zest, and juice until well combined.
3. In a separate bowl, mix the almond flour, whole wheat flour, baking powder, and sea salt.
4. Gradually fold the dry ingredients into the wet mixture, stirring until smooth.
5. Pour the batter into the prepared pan and bake for 35-40 minutes, or until a toothpick inserted into the center comes out clean.
6. Let the cake cool completely before serving.

Tips:
- For a gluten-free version, use all almond flour or a gluten-free flour blend.
- Try using yacon syrup or monk fruit syrup for an even lighter sweetness.
- Add a pinch of cinnamon for a cozy twist.

Ingredients:

- 1 ¼ cups almond flour
- ½ cup whole wheat flour (or gluten-free flour)
- ¾ cup olive oil
- ⅓ cup date syrup or coconut nectar (for a lower glycemic option)
- 3 eggs
- Zest of 1 orange
- Juice of 1 orange
- 1 teaspoon baking powder
- ¼ teaspoon sea salt

Nutrition per macaroon:

- Calories: 270
- Protein: 6g
- Carbohydrates: 23g
- Fats: 18g
- Fiber: 3g
- Cholesterol: 55mg
- Sodium: 130mg
- Potassium: 120mg

Cacao and Almond Butter Bites

 PREP TIME 10 MIN    **CHILL TIME** 20 MIN    **YIELD** 12 BITES

Instructions:

1. Mix almond butter, cocoa powder, coconut flour, honey, chia seeds, and sea salt in a bowl until a dough forms.
2. Roll the mixture into small balls and place on a parchment-lined tray.
3. Freeze for 20 minutes to firm up. Serve chilled.

Tips:
- Replace almond butter with peanut butter or cashew butter for different flavors.
- Use cacao powder instead of unsweetened cocoa powder for a deeper chocolate taste.
- Add hemp seeds for an extra boost of protein.

Ingredients:

- ½ cup almond butter
- 2 tablespoons unsweetened cocoa powder
- 2 tablespoons coconut flour
- 2 tablespoons honey or maple syrup
- 1 tablespoon chia seeds
- Pinch of sea salt

Nutrition per bite:

Calories: 90 | Protein: 3g | Carbohydrates: 7g | Fats: 6g | Fiber: 2g | Cholesterol: 0mg | Sodium: 20mg | Potassium: 90mg

---

Fig and Walnut Stuffed Dates

 PREP TIME 10 MIN   **YIELD** 12 SERVINGS

Instructions:

1. Slice open each date and gently remove the pit.
2. In a small bowl, mix the chopped figs, cinnamon, and almond butter (if using).
3. Stuff each date with a walnut half and a small spoonful of the fig mixture.
4. Press closed and serve immediately or refrigerate until ready to eat.

Tips:
- Use pecans or almonds instead of walnuts for a different texture.
- Swap dried figs with dried apricots for a sweeter filling.
- Add a sprinkle of sea salt on top for a sweet-salty contrast.

Ingredients:

- 12 large Medjool dates, pitted
- 12 walnut halves
- 6 dried figs, chopped
- 1 teaspoon cinnamon
- 1 tablespoon almond butter (optional)

Nutrition per Serving:

Calories: 120 | Protein: 2g | Carbohydrates: 22g | Fats: 3g | Fiber: 3g | Cholesterol: 0mg | Sodium: 0mg | Potassium: 230mg

Mint Chocolate Avocado Brownies

PREP TIME 10 MIN   **COOK TIME** 25 MIN   **YIELD** 9 SERVINGS

Instructions:

1. Preheat the oven to 350°F (175°C). Grease an 8x8 baking dish.
2. Combine the avocado, cocoa powder, maple syrup, eggs, peppermint extract, baking powder, and sea salt in a blender until smooth.
3. Stir in the almond flour and fold in the dark chocolate chips.
4. Pour the batter into the prepared baking dish and smooth the top.
5. Bake for 20-25 minutes, until a toothpick comes out clean. Let cool before slicing.

Tips:
- Replace almond flour with oat flour for a nut-free version.
- Use vanilla extract instead of peppermint if you prefer a classic chocolate flavor.
- Swap avocado with mashed banana for a sweeter base.

Ingredients:

- 1 ripe avocado
- ½ cup cocoa powder
- ½ cup almond flour
- ¼ cup maple syrup
- 2 eggs (or flax eggs for vegan)
- 1 teaspoon peppermint extract
- 1 teaspoon baking powder
- ¼ teaspoon sea salt
- ¼ cup dark chocolate chips (optional)

Nutrition per Serving:

- Calories: 180
- Protein: 4g
- Carbohydrates: 16g
- Fats: 11g
- Fiber: 4g
- Cholesterol: 35mg
- Sodium: 100mg
- Potassium: 250mg

Cardamom Poached Pears with Pistachios

 **PREP TIME** 10 MIN    **COOK TIME** 20 MIN   **YIELD** 4 SERVINGS

Instructions:

1. In a large saucepan, bring the water, honey, cardamom pods, cinnamon stick, and lemon juice to a boil.
2. Reduce heat to low and gently add the pears to the poaching liquid.
3. Simmer for 15-20 minutes, turning the pears occasionally until they are tender but still hold their shape.
4. Remove the pears from the liquid and let them cool slightly.
5. Serve the pears warm or chilled, topped with chopped pistachios.

Tips:
- Use almonds or walnuts instead of pistachios for a different nutty topping.
- Add a few saffron strands to the poaching liquid for a deeper flavor.

Ingredients:

- 4 ripe but firm pears, peeled and cored
- 4 cups water
- ¼ cup honey or maple syrup
- 4 cardamom pods, lightly crushed
- 1 cinnamon stick
- ¼ cup chopped pistachios
- 1 teaspoon lemon juice

Nutrition per Serving:

Calories: 160 | Protein: 2g | Carbohydrates: 34g | Fats: 3g | Fiber: 6g | Cholesterol: 0mg | Sodium: 10mg | Potassium: 280mg

---

Blueberry Coconut Macaroons

 PREP TIME 10 MIN   **COOK TIME** 15 MIN   **YIELD** 12 MACAROONS

Instructions:

1. Preheat the oven to 350°F (175°C) and line a baking sheet with parchment paper.
2. In a bowl, mix the shredded coconut, almond flour, and mashed blueberries.
3. Add the stevia, vanilla extract, and melted coconut oil, stirring until combined.
4. Form the mixture into small balls and place them on the baking sheet.
5. Bake for 12-15 minutes until golden on the edges.
6. Cool completely before serving.

Tips:
- Use raspberries or blackberries instead of blueberries.
- Replace almond flour with coconut flour or oat flour for a grain-free or nut-free option.
- Add a drizzle of melted dark chocolate for extra richness.

Ingredients:

- 1 ½ cups shredded unsweetened coconut
- ¼ cup almond flour
- 3-4 drops liquid stevia (or ¼ teaspoon stevia powder, adjust to taste)
- 1 teaspoon vanilla extract
- ¼ cup fresh or frozen blueberries, mashed slightly
- 1 tablespoon coconut oil, melted

Nutrition per macaroon:

Calories: 90 | Protein: 2g | Carbohydrates: 6g | Fats: 8g | Fiber: 3g | Cholesterol: 0mg | Sodium: 10mg | Potassium: 80mg

Banana and Walnut Muffins (Gluten-Free)

 PREP TIME
10 MIN

COOK TIME
25 MIN

YIELD
12 SERVINGS

Instructions:

1. Preheat the oven to 350°F (175°C) and line a muffin tin with paper liners.
2. Whisk together the mashed bananas, eggs, coconut oil, maple syrup, and vanilla extract in a large bowl.
3. Combine the almond flour, baking soda, cinnamon, and salt in another bowl.
4. Add the dry ingredients to the wet ingredients and stir until well combined. Fold in the chopped walnuts.
5. Spoon the batter into the muffin tin, filling each cup about ¾ full.
6. Bake for 20-25 minutes, or until a toothpick inserted into the center comes out clean.
7. Let cool before serving.

Tips:
- Replace walnuts with pecans or chopped almonds for a different crunch.
- Use applesauce instead of bananas for a different flavor.
- Swap maple syrup for agave or date syrup for a different natural sweetener.

Ingredients:

- 2 ripe bananas, mashed
- 2 eggs
- ¼ cup coconut oil, melted
- ¼ cup maple syrup or honey
- 1 teaspoon vanilla extract
- 1 ½ cups almond flour
- ½ teaspoon baking soda
- 1 teaspoon cinnamon
- ¼ cup chopped walnuts
- Pinch of sea salt

Nutrition per Serving:

- Calories: 190
- Protein: 4g
- Carbohydrates: 12g
- Fats: 15g
- Fiber: 3g
- Cholesterol: 35mg
- Sodium: 95mg
- Potassium: 160mg

Pumpkin and Chia Seed Parfait

 PREP TIME
10 MIN

 CHILL TIME
2 HOUR

 YIELD
4 SERVINGS

Ingredients:

- 1 cup unsweetened pumpkin purée
- 1 ½ cups almond milk (or other plant-based milk)
- 4 tablespoons chia seeds
- 2 tablespoons maple syrup or honey
- 1 teaspoon vanilla extract
- 1 teaspoon cinnamon
- ¼ teaspoon nutmeg
- ¼ cup chopped walnuts or pecans (optional)

Nutrition per Serving:

- Calories: 180
- Protein: 4g
- Carbohydrates: 19g
- Fats: 9g
- Fiber: 8g
- Cholesterol: 0mg
- Sodium: 25mg
- Potassium: 350mg

Instructions:

1. Whisk together the almond milk, chia seeds, maple syrup, vanilla extract, cinnamon, and nutmeg in a bowl.
2. Refrigerate for at least 2 hours (or overnight), stirring occasionally to prevent clumping, until the chia seeds form a pudding-like consistency.
3. Layer the chia pudding and pumpkin purée in serving glasses to assemble the parfaits.
4. Top with chopped walnuts or pecans for added crunch, if desired.
5. Serve chilled and enjoy!

Tips:
- Use coconut milk for a richer version of the parfait.
- Swap pumpkin with sweet potato purée for a slightly different flavor.
- Replace maple syrup with agave syrup or date syrup for a lower-glycemic sweetener.

Sweet Potato Brownies

 PREP TIME **15 MIN**  **COOK TIME** **30 MIN**  **YIELD** **9 SERVINGS**

Instructions:

1. Preheat the oven to 350°F (175°C) and line an 8x8 inch baking pan with parchment paper.
2. Mix the mashed sweet potato, almond butter, maple syrup, and vanilla extract in a bowl.
3. Add the cocoa powder, baking powder, and salt, and stir until the batter is smooth.
4. Pour the batter into the prepared baking pan and smooth the top.
5. Bake for 25-30 minutes, or until a toothpick inserted into the center comes out clean.
6. Let cool completely before cutting into squares.

Tips:
- Replace almond butter with peanut butter or cashew butter.
- Add chocolate chips or nuts for extra texture.
- Use honey instead of maple syrup for a different sweetness.

Ingredients:

- 1 cup mashed sweet potato (cooked and peeled)
- ¼ cup almond butter
- ¼ cup cocoa powder
- ¼ cup maple syrup
- 1 teaspoon vanilla extract
- ½ teaspoon baking powder
- Pinch of salt

Nutrition per Serving:

- Calories: 110
- Protein: 3g
- Carbohydrates: 18g
- Fats: 5g
- Fiber: 2g
- Cholesterol: 0mg
- Sodium: 50mg
- Potassium: 230mg

Almond Flour Lemon Cookies

 PREP TIME 10 MIN    **COOK TIME** 12 MIN    **YIELD** 12 COOKIES

Instructions:

1. Preheat the oven to 350°F (175°C) and line a baking sheet with parchment paper.
2. Mix the almond flour, baking soda, and salt in a bowl.
3. Whisk together the coconut oil, maple syrup, lemon zest, lemon juice, and vanilla extract in another bowl.
4. Combine the wet and dry ingredients, mixing until a dough forms.
5. Roll the dough into small balls and place them on the prepared baking sheet, gently flattening them.
6. Bake for 10-12 minutes or until the edges are golden.
7. Let cool on the baking sheet before transferring to a wire rack.

Ingredients:

- 1 ½ cups almond flour
- ¼ cup coconut oil, melted
- ¼ cup maple syrup or honey
- 1 tablespoon lemon zest
- 1 tablespoon fresh lemon juice
- 1 teaspoon vanilla extract
- ¼ teaspoon baking soda
- Pinch of sea salt

Nutrition per cookie:

- Calories: 140
- Protein: 3g
- Carbohydrates: 8g
- Fats: 11g
- Fiber: 2g
- Cholesterol: 0mg
- Sodium: 35mg
- Potassium: 45mg

Tips:
- Replace maple syrup with agave syrup or date syrup for a different sweetness.
- Use orange zest and juice for an orange-flavored variation.
- Add poppy seeds for a lemon poppy seed twist.

40

Blueberry Coconut Crisp

⏱ PREP TIME
10 MIN

🍳 COOK TIME
30 MIN

🍽 YIELD
6 SERVINGS

Instructions:

1. Preheat the oven to 350°F (175°C).
2. In a large bowl, mix blueberries, lemon juice, stevia, and vanilla extract. Pour the mixture into a baking dish.
3. In a separate bowl, combine shredded coconut, oats, almond flour, melted coconut oil, cinnamon, and salt.
4. Spread the coconut-oat mixture evenly over the blueberries.
5. Bake for 25-30 minutes until the topping is golden brown and the blueberries are bubbling.
6. Let cool slightly before serving. Serve warm with coconut yogurt or dairy-free ice cream, if desired.

Tips:
- Use raspberries or blackberries instead of blueberries.
- Replace almond flour with oat flour for a nut-free option.
- Add chopped nuts like pecans or almonds for extra crunch.

Ingredients:

- 4 cups fresh or frozen blueberries
- 1 tablespoon lemon juice
- 3-4 drops liquid stevia (or ¼ teaspoon stevia powder, adjust to taste)
- 1 teaspoon vanilla extract
- 1 cup shredded unsweetened coconut
- ½ cup rolled oats
- ¼ cup almond flour
- ¼ cup coconut oil, melted
- 1 teaspoon cinnamon
- Pinch of sea salt

Nutrition per Serving:

- Calories: 180
- Protein: 2g
- Carbohydrates: 18g
- Fats: 11g
- Fiber: 5g
- Cholesterol: 0mg
- Sodium: 20mg
- Potassium: 180mg

Pumpkin Spice Energy Balls

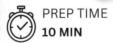 PREP TIME
10 MIN

 CHILL TIME
30 MIN

 YIELD
12 BALLS

Instructions:

1. In a large bowl, mix rolled oats, almond butter, pumpkin puree, stevia, vanilla extract, pumpkin spice, ground flaxseeds, and chopped nuts.
2. Stir until well combined.
3. Form the mixture into 1-inch balls.
4. Refrigerate for at least 30 minutes to set before serving.

Tips:
- Use peanut butter or cashew butter instead of almond butter for variety.
- Replace ground flaxseeds with chia seeds for extra fiber.
- Add dark chocolate chips for a touch of indulgence.

Ingredients:

- 1 cup rolled oats
- ½ cup almond butter
- ⅓ cup pumpkin puree
- 2-3 drops liquid stevia (or ⅛ teaspoon stevia powder, adjust to taste)
- 1 teaspoon vanilla extract
- 1 teaspoon pumpkin spice mix
- ¼ cup ground flaxseeds
- ¼ cup chopped walnuts or pecans

Nutrition per ball:

Calories: 120 | Protein: 3g | Carbohydrates: 8g | Fats: 8g | Fiber: 3g | Cholesterol: 0mg | Sodium: 10mg | Potassium: 130mg

---

Lemon Chia Bars

 PREP TIME
15 MIN

 CHILL TIME
1 HOUR

 YIELD
12 BARS

Instructions:

1. Mix the almond flour, shredded coconut, and chia seeds in a bowl.
2. Add the maple syrup, melted coconut oil, lemon zest, lemon juice, and sea salt, stirring until well combined.
3. Press the mixture evenly into a lined 8x8-inch baking dish.
4. Refrigerate for at least 1 hour until firm.
5. Cut into squares and serve chilled.

Tips:
- Replace chia seeds with flaxseeds for a similar nutritional profile.
- Use lime juice and zest instead of lemon for a tangy twist.
- Add slivered almonds or pistachios to the base for extra texture.

Ingredients:

- 1½ cups almond flour
- ½ cup shredded unsweetened coconut
- ¼ cup chia seeds
- 2 tablespoons maple syrup or honey
- 2 tablespoons coconut oil, melted
- Zest and juice of 1 lemon
- Pinch of sea salt

Nutrition per bar:

Calories: 150 | Protein: 4g | Carbohydrates: 9g | Fats: 12g | Fiber: 5g | Cholesterol: 0mg | Sodium: 20mg | Potassium: 110mg

Coconut Rice Pudding

 **PREP TIME** 5 MIN  **COOK TIME** 25 MIN  **YIELD** 4 SERVINGS

Instructions:

1. Combine the cooked rice, coconut milk, maple syrup, vanilla, cinnamon, and sea salt in a medium saucepan.
2. Cook over medium heat, stirring frequently, for 20-25 minutes, until the mixture thickens and becomes creamy.
3. Remove from heat and let cool slightly before serving.
4. Serve warm or chilled, topped with fresh fruit or toasted coconut if desired.

Ingredients:

- 1 cup cooked jasmine or basmati rice
- 1½ cups coconut milk (full-fat or light)
- 2 tablespoons maple syrup or honey
- 1 teaspoon vanilla extract
- ¼ teaspoon cinnamon
- Pinch of sea salt
- Fresh fruit or toasted coconut for topping (optional)

Tips:
- Replace white rice with brown rice for a higher-fiber version.
- Use almond or oat milk instead of coconut milk for a lighter texture.
- Add a pinch of nutmeg or cardamom for additional warmth.

Nutrition per Serving:

- Calories: 220
- Protein: 3g
- Carbohydrates: 29g
- Fats: 11g
- Fiber: 1g
- Cholesterol: 0mg
- Sodium: 55mg
- Potassium: 180mg

Roasted Figs with Balsamic and Honey

 PREP TIME
5 MIN

 COOK TIME
15 MIN

 YIELD
4 SERVINGS

Instructions:

1. Preheat the oven to 400°F (200°C).
2. Arrange the halved figs on a baking sheet, cut side up.
3. Drizzle with balsamic vinegar and honey, making sure each fig gets evenly coated.
4. Roast in the oven for 12-15 minutes, until the figs are tender and slightly caramelized.
5. Remove from the oven and sprinkle with thyme leaves and chopped walnuts, if using.
6. Serve warm as a dessert or alongside yogurt or cheese.

Ingredients:

- 8 fresh figs, halved
- 2 tablespoons balsamic vinegar
- 2 tablespoons honey (or maple syrup)
- 1 teaspoon fresh thyme leaves (optional)
- ¼ cup chopped walnuts (optional)

Nutrition per Serving:

Calories: 140 | Protein: 2g |
Carbohydrates: 24g | Fats: 4g | Fiber: 3g |
Cholesterol: 0mg | Sodium: 10mg |
Potassium: 270mg

Tips:
- Use maple syrup instead of honey for a vegan version.
- Replace balsamic vinegar with pomegranate molasses for a deeper, tangier flavor.
- Add a sprinkle of sea salt for a sweet and salty contrast.

Peach and Basil Granita

 PREP TIME
10 MIN

 CHILL TIME
3 HOUR

 YIELD
4 SERVINGS

Instructions:

1. Combine the peaches, basil, honey, lemon juice, and water in a blender. Blend until smooth.
2. Pour the mixture into a shallow dish and place it in the freezer.
3. Every 30 minutes, scrape the mixture with a fork to create a granita texture. Repeat scraping every 30 minutes for about 3 hours until the granita is fully frozen and fluffy.
4. Serve immediately, garnished with extra basil leaves.

Ingredients:

- 4 ripe peaches, peeled and chopped
- ¼ cup fresh basil leaves
- 2 tablespoons honey or maple syrup
- Juice of 1 lemon
- ½ cup water

Nutrition per Serving:

Calories: 90 | Protein: 1g |
Carbohydrates:23g | Fats: 0g | Fiber: 3g |
Cholesterol: 0mg | Sodium: 5mg |
Potassium: 250mg

Tips:
- Replace peaches with nectarines or mangoes for a tropical twist.
- Use mint instead of basil for a refreshing alternative.
- Add a pinch of ginger for an extra layer of flavor.

Carrot Cake Bites

 PREP TIME
15 MIN

 CHILL TIME
30 MIN

 YIELD
12 BITES

Instructions:

1. In a food processor, pulse the rolled oats until they resemble coarse flour.
2. Add the grated carrots, dates, almond flour, shredded coconut, cinnamon, nutmeg, ginger, almond butter, and vanilla extract to the processor.
3. Blend until the mixture comes together into a dough-like consistency.
4. Scoop and roll the mixture into bite-sized balls.
5. Chill in the refrigerator for about 30 minutes before serving.

Ingredients:

- 1 cup grated carrots
- 1 cup rolled oats
- ½ cup almond flour
- ½ cup Medjool dates, pitted
- ¼ cup shredded coconut
- 1 teaspoon cinnamon
- ½ teaspoon nutmeg
- ¼ teaspoon ground ginger
- 1 tablespoon almond butter
- 1 teaspoon vanilla extract

Tips:
- Swap almond flour with coconut flour for a nut-free option.
- Replace Medjool dates with raisins or dried apricots.
- Add chopped walnuts or pecans for extra crunch.

Nutrition per bite:

- Calories: 80
- Protein: 2g
- Carbohydrates: 12g
- Fats: 3g
- Fiber: 2g
- Cholesterol: 0mg
- Sodium: 10mg
- Potassium: 130mg

Black Sesame and Coconut Ice Cream

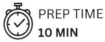 PREP TIME
10 MIN

 CHILL TIME
4 HOURS

 YIELD
4 SERVINGS

Instructions:

1. In a blender, combine the coconut milk, toasted black sesame seeds, maple syrup, vanilla extract, and coconut oil.
2. Blend until smooth and creamy.
3. Pour the mixture into a freezer-safe container and freeze for 3-4 hours, stirring every hour to prevent large ice crystals from forming.
4. Once frozen, scoop into bowls and serve.

Tips:
- Use white sesame seeds if you can't find black sesame seeds, though the flavor will be milder.
- Replace maple syrup with coconut sugar for a more caramel-like sweetness.
- Add a dash of ground cardamom for a warm, fragrant twist.

Ingredients:

- 1 can full-fat coconut milk
- ¼ cup black sesame seeds, toasted
- 2 tablespoons maple syrup or honey
- 1 teaspoon vanilla extract
- 1 tablespoon coconut oil

Nutrition per Serving:

Calories: 210 | Protein: 2g |
Carbohydrates: 10g | Fats: 18g | Fiber: 2g |
Cholesterol: 0mg | Sodium: 15mg |
Potassium: 180mg

Tahini and Date Bliss Balls

 PREP TIME
15 MIN

 CHILL TIME
30 MIN

 YIELD
12 SERVINGS

Instructions:

1. In a food processor, combine the dates, tahini, oats, chia seeds, vanilla extract, and cocoa powder (if using).
2. Process until the mixture is smooth and sticky.
3. Roll the mixture into 1-inch balls and coat them in shredded coconut, if desired.
4. Chill in the refrigerator for at least 30 minutes before serving.

Tips:
- Use almond butter or peanut butter instead of tahini for a different flavor.
- Replace dates with dried apricots or raisins for variety.
- Add a pinch of sea salt for a sweet-salty combination.

Ingredients:

- 1 cup pitted Medjool dates
- ½ cup tahini
- ½ cup oats (use gluten-free if needed)
- ¼ cup shredded coconut (optional)
- 1 tablespoon chia seeds
- 1 teaspoon vanilla extract
- 1 tablespoon cocoa powder (optional)

Nutrition per Serving:

Calories: 120 | Protein: 3g |
Carbohydrates: 18g | Fats: 5g | Fiber: 3g |
Cholesterol: 0mg | Sodium: 10mg |
Potassium: 170mg

Coconut Water and Pineapple Jelly

 **PREP TIME** **10 MIN**    **CHILL TIME** **2 HOURS**    **YIELD** **4 SERVINGS**

Instructions:

1. In a small saucepan, warm 1 cup of coconut water over low heat (do not boil).
2. Sprinkle the gelatin powder over the warmed coconut water and stir until fully dissolved.
3. Remove from heat and add the remaining coconut water, pineapple juice, and honey. Stir well.
4. Pour the mixture into individual molds or a shallow dish.
5. Refrigerate for about 2 hours until set.
6. Serve garnished with pineapple chunks.

Tips:
- Swap pineapple juice with mango or orange juice for a different flavor.
- Use agar-agar as a plant-based alternative to gelatin.
- Add mint leaves or lime zest for a fresh touch.

Ingredients:

- 2 cups coconut water
- 1 cup pineapple juice
- 2 tablespoons honey or maple syrup
- 2 tablespoons gelatin powder
- ¼ cup pineapple chunks for garnish

Nutrition per Serving:

- Calories: 70
- Protein: 2g
- Carbohydrates: 14g
- Fats: 0g
- Fiber: 1g
- Cholesterol: 0mg
- Sodium: 40mg
- Potassium: 150mg

Chilled Melon Soup with Mint

 PREP TIME
10 MIN

 CHILL TIME
1 HOURS

 YIELD
4 SERVINGS

Instructions:

1. Combine the melon cubes, lime juice, honey, and coconut water in a blender. Blend until smooth.
2. Chill the mixture in the refrigerator for at least 1 hour to allow the flavors to develop.
3. Serve cold in bowls, garnished with fresh mint leaves.

Tips:
- Use watermelon for a sweeter flavor, or mix different melons for variety.
- Replace lime juice with lemon juice for a citrusy zing.
- Add a pinch of ground ginger or cayenne pepper for a spicy twist.

Ingredients:
- 2 cups honeydew or cantaloupe melon, cubed
- Juice of 1 lime
- 1 tablespoon honey or maple syrup
- ½ cup coconut water
- Fresh mint leaves for garnish

Nutrition per Serving:

Calories: 70 | Protein: 1g | Carbohydrates:18g | Fats: 0g | Fiber: 1g | Cholesterol: 0mg | Sodium: 10mg | Potassium: 220mg

Cucumber and Lime Granita

 PREP TIME
10 MIN

 CHILL TIME
3 HOURS

 YIELD
4 SERVINGS

Instructions:

1. Blend the chopped cucumber, lime juice, honey, and water in a blender until smooth.
2. Pour the mixture into a shallow dish and place it in the freezer.
3. Every 30 minutes, scrape the mixture with a fork to create a granita texture. Continue scraping for about 3 hours or until the granita is frozen and fluffy.
4. Serve immediately, garnished with fresh mint leaves if desired.

Tips:
- Use agave syrup instead of honey for a vegan option.
- Add a dash of ginger juice for a spicy kick.
- Swap lime with lemon for a slightly different citrus flavor.

Ingredients:
- 2 large cucumbers, peeled and chopped
- Juice of 2 limes
- 2 tablespoons honey or maple syrup
- ½ cup water
- Fresh mint leaves for garnish (optional)

Nutrition per Serving:

Calories: 50 | Protein: 1g | Carbohydrates:13g | Fats: 0g | Fiber: 1g | Cholesterol: 0mg | Sodium: 10mg | Potassium: 120mg

Walnut and Apple Spice Cake (Gluten-Free)

 **PREP TIME** 20 MIN  **COOK TIME** 40 MIN  **YIELD** 8 SERVINGS

Instructions:

1. Preheat the oven to 350°F (175°C) and grease a cake pan.
2. In a bowl, combine almond flour, oat flour, baking powder, cinnamon, and nutmeg.
3. In a separate bowl, mix applesauce, maple syrup, vanilla, and eggs.
4. Gradually fold the wet mixture into the dry ingredients, then add apples and walnuts.
5. Pour the batter into the cake pan and bake for 35-40 minutes.
6. Let cool before serving.

Ingredients:

- 1 cup almond flour
- ½ cup oat flour
- 1 teaspoon baking powder
- 1 teaspoon cinnamon
- ¼ teaspoon nutmeg
- ¼ cup applesauce (unsweetened)
- ¼ cup maple syrup or 1 teaspoon stevia (optional)
- 1 teaspoon vanilla extract
- 2 eggs
- 1 cup chopped apple
- ¼ cup chopped walnuts

Nutrition per Serving:

- Calories: 190
- Protein: 5g
- Carbohydrates: 16g
- Fats: 12g
- Fiber: 3g
- Cholesterol: 40mg
- Sodium: 60mg
- Potassium: 120mg

Tips:
- Use pear instead of apple for a twist.
- Swap walnuts for pecans or almonds.
- Add 1 tablespoon of chia seeds for added fiber.

Date and Walnut Brownies

 PREP TIME
15 MIN

 COOK TIME
20 MIN

 YIELD
12 BROWNIES

Instructions:

1. Preheat oven to 350°F (175°C) and line a square baking dish with parchment paper.
2. In a food processor, blend dates until they form a paste.
3. Add eggs, cocoa powder, almond flour, vanilla, baking powder, and salt. Blend until smooth.
4. Stir in chopped walnuts and pour the batter into the prepared baking dish.
5. Bake for 20 minutes or until a toothpick comes out clean. Let cool before slicing.

Ingredients:

- 1 cup Medjool dates, pitted
- ½ cup almond flour
- ¼ cup cocoa powder
- 2 eggs
- ¼ cup walnuts, chopped
- 1 teaspoon vanilla extract
- 1 teaspoon baking powder
- Pinch of sea salt

Nutrition per brownie:

- Calories: 110
- Protein: 3g
- Carbohydrates: 15g
- Fats: 5g
- Fiber: 3g
- Cholesterol: 30mg
- Sodium: 45mg
- Potassium: 170mg

Tips:
- Replace dates with mashed bananas for a lower-sugar option.
- Use pecans or hazelnuts instead of walnuts for a different flavor.
- Add dark chocolate chips for extra richness.

Apple Cinnamon Oatmeal Cookies

 **PREP TIME** **10 MIN**    **COOK TIME** **15 MIN**    **YIELD** **12 COOKIES**

Instructions:

1. Preheat the oven to 350°F (175°C) and line a baking sheet with parchment paper.
2. In a bowl, mix rolled oats, almond flour, applesauce, honey, cinnamon, baking powder, and raisins or walnuts until combined.
3. Drop spoonfuls of the mixture onto the prepared baking sheet and flatten slightly.
4. Bake for 12-15 minutes until golden. Let cool before serving.

Ingredients:

- 1 cup rolled oats
- 1/2 cup almond flour
- 1/2 cup unsweetened applesauce
- 1/4 cup honey or stevia to taste
- 1 teaspoon cinnamon
- 1/2 teaspoon baking powder
- 1/4 cup raisins or chopped walnuts (optional)

Nutrition per cookie:

- Calories: 90
- Protein: 3g
- Carbohydrates: 15g
- Fats: 3g
- Fiber: 2g
- Cholesterol: 0mg
- Sodium: 10mg
- Potassium: 100mg

Tips:
- Substitute almond flour with oat flour for a nut-free version.
- Add chopped apples for extra texture.
- Use maple syrup instead of honey for a different sweetness.

Avocado Chocolate Truffles

 PREP TIME
10 MIN

 CHILL TIME
1 HOURS

YIELD
12 TRUFFLES

Instructions:

1. In a bowl, mix mashed avocado, cacao powder, honey, and vanilla extract until smooth.
2. Form mixture into small balls, about 1 inch in diameter.
3. Roll truffles in shredded coconut or additional cacao powder.
4. Chill for 1 hour before serving.

Tips:
- Add a dash of espresso powder for a mocha flavor.
- Use almond butter for added creaminess.
- Roll in crushed nuts for a crunchy coating.

Ingredients:

- 1 ripe avocado, mashed
- 2 tablespoons cacao powder
- 2 tablespoons honey or stevia to taste
- ½ teaspoon vanilla extract
- Unsweetened shredded coconut or cacao powder for rolling

Nutrition per truffle:

Calories: 50 | Protein: 1g | Carbohydrates:4g | Fats: 4g | Fiber: 2g | Cholesterol: 0mg | Sodium: 2mg | Potassium: 150mg

Cacao Chia Pudding with Almond Milk

 PREP TIME
5 MIN

 CHILL TIME
OVERNIGHT

 YIELD
4 SERVINGS

Instructions:

1. In a bowl, whisk almond milk, cacao powder, honey, and vanilla extract.
2. Stir in chia seeds until evenly distributed.
3. Refrigerate overnight. Stir before serving and top with fresh berries or nuts if desired.

Ingredients:

- 2 cups unsweetened almond milk
- ¼ cup chia seeds
- 2 tablespoons cacao powder
- 1-2 tablespoons honey or stevia to taste
- 1 teaspoon vanilla extract

Nutrition per Serving:

Calories: 90 | Protein: 2g | Carbohydrates: 9g | Fats: 5g | Fiber: 6g | Cholesterol: 0mg | Sodium: 5mg | Potassium: 180mg

Tips:
- Replace cacao with matcha powder for a green tea flavor.
- Use coconut milk for a creamier texture.
- Add a pinch of cinnamon for a warming note.

Caramelized Fig and Ricotta Tart

PREP TIME 15 MIN

COOK TIME 25 MIN

YIELD 8 SERVINGS

Instructions:

1. Preheat the oven to 400°F (200°C). Roll out the puff pastry and place it in a tart pan.
2. In a bowl, mix ricotta cheese, honey, vanilla extract, and sea salt until smooth. Spread evenly in the pastry.
3. Arrange the halved figs on top of the ricotta mixture, cut side up.
4. Bake for 20-25 minutes until the pastry is golden and the figs are caramelized. Serve warm or at room temperature.

Ingredients:

- 1 sheet whole wheat puff pastry (or gluten-free alternative)
- 8 fresh figs, halved
- 1 tablespoon honey or maple syrup
- 1 cup ricotta cheese
- 1 teaspoon vanilla extract
- Pinch of sea salt

Tips:
- Use pears or peaches instead of figs.
- Replace ricotta with Greek yogurt for a tangy flavor.
- Drizzle with balsamic glaze for a gourmet touch.

Nutrition per Serving:

- Calories: 200
- Protein: 6g
- Carbohydrates: 25g
- Fats: 10g
- Fiber: 3g
- Cholesterol: 20mg
- Sodium: 80mg
- Potassium: 150mg

Sugar-Free Meringues

 PREP TIME
10 MIN

 COOK TIME
2 HOURS

YIELD
10 MERINGUES

Instructions:

1. Preheat the oven to 200°F (90°C) and line a baking sheet with parchment paper.
2. In a clean, dry bowl, beat the egg whites on medium speed until frothy.
3. Add cream of tartar and continue beating until soft peaks form.
4. Gradually add the erythritol, 1 tablespoon at a time, and beat until stiff peaks form.
5. Add vanilla extract and mix briefly to incorporate.
6. Spoon or pipe small mounds of meringue onto the prepared baking sheet.
7. Bake for 1.5 to 2 hours or until meringues are dry to the touch. Let cool completely before serving.

Ingredients:

- 3 large egg whites
- ¼ teaspoon cream of tartar
- ¼ cup erythritol (or monk fruit sweetener)
- 1 teaspoon vanilla extract

Nutrition per meringue:

- Calories: 10
- Protein: 1g
- Carbohydrates: 0g
- Fats: 0g
- Fiber: 0g
- Sodium: 10mg
- Potassium: 15mg

Tips:
- Use a pinch of salt to enhance the flavor.
- Try adding a drop of almond or lemon extract for a flavor twist.
- Store in an airtight container to keep meringues crisp.

No-Bake Coconut Fat Bombs

 **PREP TIME**
10 MIN

 **CHILL TIME**
30 MIN

 **YIELD**
10 FAT BOMBS

Instructions:

1. In a mixing bowl, combine melted coconut oil, shredded coconut, coconut flour, monk fruit sweetener, and vanilla extract.
2. Mix well until ingredients are fully combined.
3. Scoop the mixture into a silicone mold or roll into small balls, then place in the freezer for 20–30 minutes until firm.
4. Store fat bombs in the fridge or freezer and enjoy as a chilled snack.

Ingredients:

- ½ cup coconut oil, melted
- ½ cup unsweetened shredded coconut
- 2 tablespoons coconut flour
- 1–2 tablespoons monk fruit sweetener (to taste)
- 1 teaspoon vanilla extract

Tips:
- Add a tablespoon of cocoa powder for a chocolate coconut flavor.
- Sprinkle with sea salt before freezing for a sweet-salty treat.
- Use almond or cashew butter for extra creaminess and flavor.

Nutrition per bomb:

- Calories: 80
- Protein: 0g
- Carbohydrates: 1g
- Fats: 8g
- Fiber: 1g
- Sodium: 5mg
- Potassium: 20mg

Nut Butter Chocolate Fudge

 PREP TIME 5 MIN    **CHILL TIME** 30 MIN    **YIELD** 12 SQUARES

Instructions:

1. In a medium bowl, combine almond butter, melted coconut oil, cocoa powder, monk fruit sweetener, vanilla extract, and salt.
2. Stir until smooth and well-mixed.
3. Pour the mixture into a lined or greased small pan and smooth the surface.
4. Freeze for 20–30 minutes until firm. Cut into squares and store in the fridge or freezer.

Ingredients:

- ½ cup almond butter (or any nut butter)
- ¼ cup coconut oil, melted
- 2 tablespoons unsweetened cocoa powder
- 1–2 tablespoons monk fruit sweetener (to taste)
- 1 teaspoon vanilla extract
- Pinch of salt

Nutrition per square:

- Calories: 120
- Protein: 2g
- Carbohydrates: 3g
- Fats: 11g
- Fiber: 1g
- Sodium: 20mg
- Potassium: 75mg

Tips:
- Use peanut butter for a richer, more intense flavor.
- Add a sprinkle of cacao nibs on top for crunch and extra antioxidants.
- Substitute cocoa powder with carob powder for a naturally sweeter taste.

Blackberry Ricotta Mousse

 PREP TIME
5 MIN

 CHILL TIME
30 MIN

 YIELD
2 SERVINGS

Instructions:

1. In a blender, combine blackberries, ricotta cheese, sweetener, and vanilla extract. Blend until smooth and creamy.
2. Pour the mousse into serving bowls and refrigerate for 30 minutes before serving.
3. Garnish with fresh blackberries and mint leaves.

Ingredients:

- 1 cup fresh blackberries
- ½ cup ricotta cheese (preferably low-fat)
- 1 tablespoon honey or monk fruit sweetener
- ½ teaspoon vanilla extract
- Fresh blackberries and mint leaves (for garnish)

Tips:
- Substitute ricotta with Greek yogurt for a tangier flavor.
- Add a splash of lemon juice to enhance the berry flavor.
- Top with a sprinkle of chia seeds for extra fiber and nutrients.

Nutrition per serving:

- Calories: 90
- Protein: 4g
- Carbohydrates: 10g
- Fats: 4g
- Fiber: 2g
- Sodium: 20mg
- Potassium: 100mg

Spiced Chai Tea Latte Pudding

 PREP TIME
10 MIN

 CHILL TIME
1 HOUR

YIELD
4 SERVINGS

Instructions:

1. In a small saucepan, heat the almond milk until warm. Add the chai tea bags and let steep for 5 minutes, then remove the tea bags.
2. In a medium bowl, whisk together the chai-infused almond milk, chia seeds, sweetener, cinnamon, ginger, and vanilla.
3. Cover and refrigerate for at least 1 hour or until thickened. Stir before serving.

Ingredients:

- 1 ½ cups unsweetened almond milk (or any plant-based milk)
- 2 chai tea bags
- 3 tablespoons chia seeds
- 1 tablespoon monk fruit sweetener (or honey)
- ½ teaspoon cinnamon
- ¼ teaspoon ground ginger
- ¼ teaspoon vanilla extract

Nutrition per serving:

- Calories: 60
- Protein: 1g
- Carbohydrates: 6g
- Fats: 4g
- Fiber: 3g
- Sodium: 20mg
- Potassium: 90mg

Tips:
- For extra creaminess, add 1 tablespoon of coconut cream to the pudding mixture.
- Serve with a sprinkle of cinnamon or a dollop of coconut whipped cream.
- Adjust the sweetness to taste if using honey or monk fruit.

No-Bake Lemon Cheesecake Balls

 **PREP TIME** 10 MIN
 **CHILL TIME** 30 MIN
 **YIELD** 12 BALLS

Instructions:

1. In a bowl, combine cream cheese, almond flour, lemon juice, lemon zest, sweetener, and vanilla extract. Mix until smooth and well combined.
2. Roll the mixture into small balls and place on a parchment-lined tray.
3. Chill in the refrigerator for at least 30 minutes before serving.

Ingredients:

- ½ cup cream cheese (preferably light), softened
- ¼ cup almond flour
- 1 tablespoon lemon juice
- 1 teaspoon lemon zest
- 1 tablespoon monk fruit sweetener (or honey)
- ½ teaspoon vanilla extract

Nutrition per ball:

- Calories: 45
- Protein: 1g
- Carbohydrates: 2g
- Fats: 4g
- Fiber: 1g
- Sodium: 15mg
- Potassium: 25mg

Tips:
- Roll the balls in shredded coconut or crushed nuts for extra texture.
- Adjust lemon juice to taste for a more intense lemon flavor.
- Store leftovers in the refrigerator for up to 3 days.

Zucchini Brownies

 PREP TIME 10 MIN  **COOK TIME** 25 MIN  **YIELD** 9 BROWNIES

Instructions:

1. Preheat the oven to 350°F (175°C) and line an 8x8-inch baking dish with parchment paper.
2. In a mixing bowl, combine grated zucchini, almond flour, cocoa powder, sweetener, coconut oil, egg, baking powder, vanilla extract, and salt. Stir until well combined.
3. Pour the batter into the prepared baking dish and spread it evenly.
4. Bake for 20–25 minutes or until a toothpick inserted into the center comes out clean. Let cool before slicing.

Ingredients:

- 1 cup grated zucchini (about 1 medium zucchini)
- ½ cup almond flour
- ¼ cup unsweetened cocoa powder
- ¼ cup monk fruit sweetener (or honey)
- 2 tablespoons coconut oil, melted
- 1 large egg (or flax egg for vegan)
- ½ teaspoon baking powder
- 1 teaspoon vanilla extract
- Pinch of salt

Nutrition per brownie:

- Calories: 90
- Protein: 2g
- Carbohydrates: 8g
- Fats: 6g
- Fiber: 2g
- Sodium: 40mg
- Potassium: 150mg

Tips:
- For extra richness, add ¼ cup of dark chocolate chips to the batter.
- Substitute almond flour with oat flour for a different texture.
- Store brownies in an airtight container in the fridge for up to a week.

Baked Pumpkin Custard

 PREP TIME
10 MIN

 COOK TIME
35 MIN

 YIELD
4 SERVINGS

Instructions:

1. Preheat the oven to 350°F (175°C) and lightly grease four ramekins or custard cups.
2. In a mixing bowl, whisk together pumpkin puree, almond milk, eggs, sweetener, vanilla, cinnamon, ginger, and nutmeg until smooth.
3. Pour the mixture evenly into the ramekins. Place the ramekins in a baking dish and add hot water to the dish to come halfway up the sides of the ramekins.
4. Bake for 35 minutes or until the custard is set. Let cool slightly before serving.

Tips:
- Serve with a sprinkle of cinnamon or a dollop of coconut whipped cream.
- For extra creaminess, use coconut milk instead of almond milk.
- Refrigerate leftovers and enjoy cold for a different flavor experience.

Ingredients:

- 1 cup pumpkin puree
- ½ cup almond milk (or any plant-based milk)
- 2 large eggs
- 2 tablespoons monk fruit sweetener (or honey)
- 1 teaspoon vanilla extract
- ½ teaspoon ground cinnamon
- ¼ teaspoon ground ginger
- ¼ teaspoon ground nutmeg

Nutrition per ball:

- Calories: 45
- Protein: 1g
- Carbohydrates: 2g
- Fats: 4g
- Fiber: 1g
- Sodium: 15mg
- Potassium: 25mg

Chocolate Espresso Balls

 PREP TIME
10 MIN

 CHILL TIME
1 HOUR

 YIELD
10 SERVINGS

Ingredients:

- 1 cup almond flour
- 2 tablespoons unsweetened cocoa powder
- 1 tablespoon instant espresso powder
- 3 tablespoons almond butter
- 2 tablespoons monk fruit sweetener (or honey)
- 1 teaspoon vanilla extract

Nutrition per serving:

- Calories: 80
- Protein: 2g
- Carbohydrates: 3g
- Fats: 7g
- Fiber: 1g
- Sodium: 5mg
- Potassium: 50mg

Instructions:

1. In a mixing bowl, combine almond flour, cocoa powder, and espresso powder.
2. Add almond butter, sweetener, and vanilla extract. Mix until a dough forms.
3. Roll the mixture into small balls and place them on a baking sheet lined with parchment paper.
4. Chill in the refrigerator for at least 1 hour before serving.

Tips:
- Substitute espresso powder with cinnamon for a chocolate-spice twist.
- Roll the balls in shredded coconut, chopped nuts, or cacao powder for extra flavor and texture.
- Store in the fridge for up to a week for a convenient snack.

Low-Carb Crème Brûlée

 PREP TIME
15 MIN

 COOK TIME
30 MIN

 CHILL TIME
2 HOURS

 YIELD
4 SERVINGS

Instructions:

1. Preheat the oven to 325°F (160°C). In a saucepan, heat the cream until warm but not boiling.
2. In a mixing bowl, whisk together egg yolks and sweetener until light in color. Gradually add the warm cream, whisking constantly. Stir in the vanilla extract.
3. Pour the mixture into small ramekins and place them in a baking dish. Add hot water to the dish, filling halfway up the sides of the ramekins.
4. Bake for 30 minutes or until the crème brûlée is set but still slightly jiggly in the center.
5. Chill in the fridge for at least 2 hours. Before serving, sprinkle with a little additional sweetener and use a kitchen torch to caramelize the top.

Tips:
- Substitute heavy cream with almond milk for a lighter version, though it will be less rich.
- Add a pinch of instant coffee granules for a subtle coffee flavor.
- If you don't have a kitchen torch, place the ramekins under the broiler to caramelize the topping.

Ingredients:

- 1 cup heavy cream (or coconut cream for dairy-free)
- 2 large egg yolks
- 2 tablespoons monk fruit sweetener (or honey)
- 1 teaspoon vanilla extract

Nutrition per serving:

- Calories: 160
- Protein: 3g
- Carbohydrates: 2g
- Fats: 15g
- Fiber: 0g
- Sodium: 15mg
- Potassium: 50mg

Vanilla and Almond Flan

 PREP TIME
10 MIN

 COOK TIME
35 MIN

 YIELD
4 SERVINGS

Ingredients:

- 1 cup unsweetened almond milk
- 3 large eggs
- 2 tablespoons monk fruit sweetener (or honey)
- 1 teaspoon vanilla extract
- ¼ teaspoon almond extract
- A pinch of salt

Nutrition per serving:

- Calories: 70
- Protein: 4g
- Carbohydrates: 5g
- Fats: 4g
- Fiber: 0g
- Sodium: 55mg
- Potassium: 50mg

Instructions:

1. Preheat the oven to 325°F (160°C) and grease four small ramekins.
2. In a mixing bowl, whisk together almond milk, eggs, sweetener, vanilla extract, almond extract, and salt until smooth.
3. Pour the mixture evenly into the ramekins and place them in a baking dish. Add hot water to the baking dish, filling halfway up the sides of the ramekins.
4. Bake for 35 minutes or until the flan is set. Allow to cool slightly before serving.

Tips:
- For added flavor, sprinkle a pinch of nutmeg or cinnamon on top before baking.
- Substitute almond milk with coconut milk for a creamier texture.
- Chill the flan in the fridge for a firmer consistency before serving.

Almond Butter Banana Ice Cream

⏱ **PREP TIME**
15 MIN

❄ **CHILL TIME**
3 HOURS

🍽 **YIELD**
4 SERVINGS

Instructions:

1. Place frozen banana slices in a blender or food processor and blend until smooth.
2. Add almond butter and vanilla extract and blend until creamy.
3. Serve immediately for a soft-serve texture or freeze for an additional hour for a firmer consistency.

Ingredients:

- 2 ripe bananas, sliced and frozen
- 2 tablespoons almond butter
- ¼ teaspoon vanilla extract

Tips:
- For a chocolate flavor, add 1 tablespoon of unsweetened cocoa powder.
- Substitute almond butter with peanut or cashew butter for a different flavor.
- Top with fresh berries or shredded coconut for added texture.

Nutrition per serving:

- Calories: 150
- Protein: 2g
- Carbohydrates: 25g
- Fats: 6g
- Fiber: 3g
- Sodium: 0mg
- Potassium: 400mg

Sugar-Free Caramel Sauce Drizzles

 PREP TIME
5 MIN

 **COOK TIME**
10 MIN

 YIELD
10 SERVINGS
(ABOUT 1 CUP)

Ingredients:

- ½ cup coconut cream
- ¼ cup monk fruit sweetener (or stevia, to taste)
- 1 tablespoon unsalted butter or coconut oil
- 1 teaspoon vanilla extract
- A pinch of sea salt

Nutrition per serving:

- Calories: 45
- Protein: 0g
- Carbohydrates: 2g
- Fats: 4g
- Fiber: 0g
- Sodium: 10mg
- Potassium: 20mg

Instructions:

1. In a small saucepan, combine coconut cream and sweetener over medium heat, stirring continuously.
2. Once it starts to simmer, add butter or coconut oil and continue to cook, stirring frequently, for about 10 minutes until the mixture thickens and turns golden.
3. Remove from heat and stir in vanilla extract and a pinch of salt.
4. Allow the sauce to cool slightly, then drizzle over desserts or store in an airtight container in the refrigerator.

Tips:

- Use almond or cashew cream as a substitute for coconut cream if desired.
- This sauce thickens as it cools; reheat gently if you need a thinner consistency.
- Drizzle over fresh fruit, liver-friendly ice cream, or chia pudding for a healthy dessert topping.

Cheesecake-Stuffed Dates

 **PREP TIME** 10 MIN  **CHILL TIME** 15 MIN  **YIELD** 8 SERVINGS

Instructions:

1. Slice each date lengthwise, but do not cut all the way through. Gently open the date and remove the pit.
2. In a small bowl, mix cream cheese, vanilla extract, and cinnamon until smooth.
3. Spoon a small amount of the cream cheese mixture into each date.
4. Sprinkle with crushed nuts and chill in the refrigerator for 15 minutes before serving.

Ingredients:

- 8 Medjool dates, pitted
- ¼ cup cream cheese (or vegan cream cheese)
- ½ teaspoon vanilla extract
- A pinch of cinnamon
- Crushed nuts (pistachios, almonds, or pecans), for topping

Tips:
- Use a touch of honey or monk fruit sweetener in the filling if you prefer a sweeter flavor.
- For a unique twist, add a bit of lemon zest to the cream cheese mixture.
- These make excellent bite-sized treats that can be stored in the refrigerator for up to three days.

Nutrition per serving:

- Calories: 70
- Protein: 1g
- Carbohydrates: 10g
- Fats: 3g
- Fiber: 1g
- Sodium: 20mg
- Potassium: 90mg

Lavender and Vanilla Coconut Milk Popsicles

 PREP TIME
10 MIN

 CHILL TIME
4 HOURS

 YIELD
6 SERVINGS

Instructions:

1. In a small saucepan, heat the coconut milk with the dried lavender over medium heat, stirring occasionally. Once it starts to simmer, remove from heat.
2. Allow the lavender to steep in the coconut milk for 5-10 minutes, then strain the milk to remove the lavender.
3. Stir in sweetener and vanilla extract, adjusting sweetness to taste.
4. Pour the mixture into popsicle molds and freeze for at least 4 hours before serving.

Ingredients:

- 1 can (13.5 oz) full-fat coconut milk
- 1 tablespoon dried culinary lavender
- 2 tablespoons monk fruit sweetener (or honey)
- 1 teaspoon vanilla extract

Nutrition per serving:

- Calories: 100
- Protein: 1g
- Carbohydrates: 3g
- Fats: 9g
- Fiber: 0g
- Sodium: 10mg
- Potassium: 130mg

Tips:

- For a fruitier version, add ¼ cup of mashed blueberries or strawberries before freezing.
- Make sure to use culinary-grade lavender, as it's safe for consumption and has a milder flavor.
- These popsicles can last in the freezer for up to two weeks, making them a refreshing liver-friendly treat on hand.

Rosewater Almond Cookies

 PREP TIME
10 MIN

 COOK TIME
15 MIN

 YIELD
12 COOKIES

Instructions:

1. Preheat the oven to 325°F (160°C) and line a baking sheet with parchment paper.
2. In a mixing bowl, combine almond flour, coconut oil, sweetener, rosewater, vanilla extract, and salt. Stir until a dough forms.
3. Scoop small balls of dough onto the baking sheet, flattening each slightly with your fingers.
4. Press a few sliced almonds onto each cookie, if desired.
5. Bake for 12-15 minutes, or until edges are golden. Allow to cool before serving.

Tips:
- Add a bit of lemon zest to the dough for a citrus twist.
- Rosewater can vary in strength; start with a small amount and add more to taste.
- Store these cookies in an airtight container for up to a week; they're great with tea or coffee.

Ingredients:

- 1 cup almond flour
- 3 tablespoons coconut oil, melted
- 2 tablespoons monk fruit sweetener (or honey)
- 1 teaspoon rosewater (adjust to taste)
- ½ teaspoon vanilla extract
- A pinch of salt
- Sliced almonds, for topping (optional)

Nutrition per cookie:

- Calories: 80
- Protein: 2g
- Carbohydrates: 2g
- Fats: 7g
- Fiber: 1g
- Sodium: 5mg
- Potassium: 30mg

Sugar-Free Banana Bread

 PREP TIME
10 MIN

 COOK TIME
45 MIN

 **YIELD**
8 SERVINGS

Instructions:

1. Preheat your oven to 350°F (175°C). Grease a loaf pan or line it with parchment paper.
2. In a large bowl, combine mashed bananas, eggs, melted coconut oil, and vanilla extract. Stir until well mixed.
3. In a separate bowl, mix almond flour, oat flour, baking soda, baking powder, cinnamon, and salt.
4. Gradually add the dry ingredients to the wet ingredients and mix until combined. Fold in nuts if desired.
5. Pour the batter into the prepared loaf pan and bake for 45-50 minutes, or until a toothpick inserted in the center comes out clean.
6. Allow to cool before slicing.

Ingredients:

- 3 ripe bananas, mashed
- 2 large eggs
- 1/4 cup melted coconut oil
- 1/2 cup almond flour
- 1 cup oat flour
- 1 teaspoon baking soda
- 1/2 teaspoon baking powder
- 1 teaspoon cinnamon
- 1/2 teaspoon vanilla extract
- 1/4 teaspoon salt
- 1/4 cup chopped walnuts or pecans (optional)

Nutrition per serving:

- Calories: 185
- Protein: 4g
- Carbohydrates: 21g
- Fat: 10g
- Fiber: 3g
- Sodium: 100mg
- Potassium: 290mg

Tips:

- Add 1-2 tablespoons of monk fruit sweetener if you prefer a slightly sweeter bread.
- Sprinkle a few chocolate chips on top before baking for a touch of richness.

Berry and Cream Cheese Muffins

 **PREP TIME**
15 MIN

 **COOK TIME**
20 MIN

 **YIELD**
12 MUFFINS

Instructions:

1. Preheat the oven to 350°F (175°C) and line a muffin tin with paper liners.
2. In a bowl, mix the almond flour, coconut flour, baking powder, and salt.
3. In a separate bowl, beat together cream cheese, eggs, melted coconut oil, almond milk, and vanilla extract until smooth.
4. Add the dry ingredients to the wet mixture and stir until well combined. Fold in berries.
5. Divide the batter evenly among the muffin cups and bake for 18-20 minutes, or until a toothpick inserted comes out clean.
6. Let cool slightly before serving.

Tips:
- Substitute almond milk with coconut milk for a creamier texture.
- Add a sprinkle of cinnamon for a warm, spicy aroma.

Ingredients:

- 1 cup mixed berries (blueberries, raspberries, etc.)
- 1 cup almond flour
- 1/2 cup coconut flour
- 1/2 cup cream cheese, softened
- 2 large eggs
- 1/4 cup coconut oil, melted
- 1/4 cup unsweetened almond milk
- 1 teaspoon vanilla extract
- 1 teaspoon baking powder
- 1/4 teaspoon salt

Nutrition per muffin:

- Calories: 160
- Protein: 5g
- Carbohydrates: 8g
- Fat: 14g
- Fiber: 3g
- Sodium: 80mg
- Potassium: 120mg

Cinnamon Roll Mug Cake

 PREP TIME
5 MIN

 COOK TIME
2 MIN
(MICROWAVE)

YIELD
1 SERVINGS

Instructions:

1. In a microwave-safe mug, mix almond flour, baking powder, and salt.
2. Stir in the coconut oil, almond milk, vanilla extract, and cinnamon until well combined.
3. Microwave on high for 1-2 minutes, or until the cake is set. Let it cool briefly.
4. Optionally, top with a drizzle of sugar-free icing or a sprinkle of cinnamon.

Ingredients:

- 3 tablespoons almond flour
- 1/4 teaspoon baking powder
- 1/4 teaspoon cinnamon
- 1 tablespoon coconut oil, melted
- 1 tablespoon unsweetened almond milk
- 1/4 teaspoon vanilla extract
- Pinch of salt

Nutrition per serving:

- Calories: 200
- Protein: 4g
- Carbohydrates: 7g
- Fat: 18g
- Fiber: 3g
- Sodium: 55mg
- Potassium: 60mg

Tips:
- For a "frosting," mix Greek yogurt with a few drops of vanilla extract and stevia, and spread on top.
- Add a few chopped nuts for extra texture.

Pecan Cinnamon Cookies

 PREP TIME
10 MIN

 COOK TIME
10 MIN

 YIELD
12 COOKIES

Instructions:

1. Preheat the oven to 350°F (175°C) and line a baking sheet with parchment paper.
2. In a bowl, mix almond flour, chopped pecans, baking powder, cinnamon, and salt.
3. Add the coconut oil, egg, and vanilla extract, stirring until a dough forms.
4. Scoop out tablespoon-sized amounts of dough, roll into balls, and flatten slightly on the baking sheet.
5. Bake for 8-10 minutes, or until the edges are golden brown. Let cool on a wire rack.

Tips:
- Add a dash of nutmeg for a spicier flavor.
- Substitute pecans with walnuts for a different texture and flavor.

Ingredients:

- 1 cup almond flour
- 1/4 cup finely chopped pecans
- 1/4 cup coconut oil, melted
- 1 large egg
- 1/4 teaspoon vanilla extract
- 1 teaspoon cinnamon
- 1/4 teaspoon baking powder
- 1/4 teaspoon salt

Nutrition per cookie:

- Calories: 125
- Protein: 3g
- Carbohydrates: 4g
- Fat: 11g
- Fiber: 2g
- Sodium: 40mg
- Potassium: 45mg

Sugar-Free Jello with Whipped Cream

 PREP TIME
5 MIN

 CHILL TIME
3 HOURS

 YIELD
4 SERVINGS

Instructions:

1. In a saucepan, bring water to a boil and remove from heat.
2. Sprinkle gelatin powder over the hot water and stir until completely dissolved.
3. Add the fruit juice, lemon juice, and sweetener. Stir well.
4. Pour the mixture into serving cups or molds. Refrigerate for 2-3 hours, or until set.
5. For the whipped cream topping, beat heavy cream or coconut cream with sweetener and vanilla extract until soft peaks form. Spoon onto each jello serving before eating.

Ingredients:

- 1 cup unsweetened fruit juice (like cranberry, pomegranate, or apple)
- 1 cup water
- 1 tablespoon unflavored gelatin powder
- 1 tablespoon lemon juice
- Stevia or monk fruit sweetener, to taste

Whipped Cream Topping:
- 1/2 cup heavy cream or coconut cream (for dairy-free)
- Stevia or monk fruit sweetener, to taste
- 1/2 teaspoon vanilla extract

Nutrition per serving:

- Calories: 35
- Protein: 2g
- Carbohydrates: 1g
- Fat: 3g
- Fiber: 0g
- Sodium: 5mg
- Potassium: 20mg

Tips:
- Use a mix of two different juices (like apple and cranberry) for a layered jello effect.
- Add fresh berries or small fruit pieces before chilling for added texture.

Cinnamon Roasted Chickpeas

 **PREP TIME** 5 MIN    **COOK TIME** 30 MIN    **YIELD** 4 SERVINGS

Instructions:

1. Preheat your oven to 400°F (200°C) and line a baking sheet with parchment paper.
2. Pat chickpeas dry with a paper towel. Transfer to a mixing bowl.
3. Add coconut oil, cinnamon, vanilla extract, sweetener, and salt. Toss to coat evenly.
4. Spread chickpeas in a single layer on the baking sheet.
5. Roast for 25-30 minutes, shaking the pan halfway through, until chickpeas are golden and crunchy.
6. Allow to cool before serving.

Tips:
- Adjust the sweetness to your taste by adding more or less sweetener.
- Try adding a pinch of nutmeg or ginger for a spicier flavor profile.

Ingredients:

- 1 can (15 oz) chickpeas, drained and rinsed
- 1 tablespoon coconut oil, melted
- 1 teaspoon cinnamon
- 1/2 teaspoon vanilla extract
- Stevia or monk fruit sweetener, to taste
- Pinch of salt

Nutrition per serving:

- Calories: 90
- Protein: 3g
- Carbohydrates: 12g
- Fat: 3g
- Fiber: 3g
- Sodium: 55mg
- Potassium: 115mg

Conclusion

As we conclude this journey through the world of delicious, liver-friendly desserts, I encourage you to embrace the possibilities that lie within these recipes. Each dish in this book has been carefully crafted to not only delight your taste buds but also support your overall health and well-being.

Using this book wisely means incorporating these tasty treats into a balanced diet. These recipes extend far beyond the boundaries of traditional desserts served after a meal; they can become scrumptious breakfasts to kickstart your day, invigorating snacks to keep your energy up, or even charming accompaniments to elevate your afternoon tea experience. Each dish offers a unique blend of flavors and textures that can delight your palate anytime.

Remember, each ingredient in these recipes has been selected for its health benefits, particularly in supporting liver health and overall wellness. By choosing natural sweeteners, incorporating antioxidant-packed fruits and nuts, and focusing on wholesome ingredients, you are taking significant steps toward enhancing your health while enjoying every bite.

Thank you for choosing this book as a part of your culinary journey. May it inspire you to create delicious meals that nourish your body and elevate your spirit. Embrace the journey, cherish sharing these delightful treats with loved ones, and joyfully celebrate the beauty of healthy eating!

Recipe Index

W

Z

Made in the USA
Columbia, SC
23 November 2024